D0853697

The
Cavalry
During the
Civil War

MICHAEL V. USCHAN

LUCENT
BOOKS®

GALE

San Diego • Detroit • New York • San Francisco • Cleveland • New Haven, Conn. • Waterville, Maine • London • Munich

To Lance J. Herdegen, Civil War
historian par excellence and a "man to ride the river with."

On cover: The Sixth Pennsylvania Cavalry, also known
as Rush's Lancers, pose with their trademark lances.

LIBRARY OF CONGRESS CATALOGING-IN-PUBLICATION DATA

Uschan, Michael V., 1948–
    The cavalry during the Civil War / by Michael V. Uschan.
        p. cm. — (The working life series)
    Includes bibliographic references and index.
    Summary: Recruiting and training the cavalry—Life in the saddle: the varied duties
of the cavalry trooper—Cavalry raiders and guerrillas—Cavalry soldiers in battle—Non-
combat life of the cavalry.
    ISBN 1-59018-175-1 (hardback : alk.paper)
    1. United States. Army. Cavalry—History—Civil War, 1861–1865—Juvenile literature.
2. Confederate States of America. Army. Cavalry—History—Juvenile literature.
3. United States—History—Civil War, 1861–1865—Cavalry operations—Juvenile literature. [1. United States. Army. Cavalry—History. 2. Confederate States of America. Army.
Cavalry—History. 3. United States—History—Civil War, 1861–1865.] I. Title. II. Series.
    E492.5.U83 2003
    973.7'4—dc21
2002011840

Printed in the United States of America

CONTENTS

FOREWORD

"The strongest bond of human sympathy outside the family relations should be one uniting all working people of all nations and tongues and kindreds."

Abraham Lincoln. 1864

Work is a common activity in which almost all people engage. It is probably the most universal of human experiences, the drive to work. As Henry Ford, inventor of the Model T said, "There will never be a system invented which will do away with the necessity of work." For many people, work takes up most of their day. They spend more time with their co-workers than family and friends. And the common goals people pursue on the job may be among the first thoughts that they have in the morning, and the last that they may have at night.

While the idea of work is universal, the way it is done and who performs it varies considerably throughout history. The story of work is inextricably tied to the history of technology, the history of culture, and the history of gender and race. When the typewriter was invented, for example, it was considered the exclusive domain of men who worked as secretaries. As women workers became more accepted, the secretarial role was gradually filled by women. Finally, with the invention of the computer, the modern secretary spends little time actually typing correspondence. Files are delivered via computer, and more time is spent on other tasks than the manual typing of correspondence and business.

This is just one example of how work brings together technology, gender, and culture. Another example is the American plantation slave. The harvesting of cotton was initially so cumbersome and time consuming that even with slaves, its profitability was doubtful. With the invention of the cotton gin, however, efficiency improved, and slavery became a viable agricultural tool. It also became a Southern tradition and institution, enough that the South was willing to go to war to preserve it.

The books in Lucent's Working Life series strive to show the intermingling of work, and its reflection in culture, technology, race, and gender. Indeed,

4

history viewed through the lens of the average worker is both enlightening and fascinating. Take the history of the typewriter, mentioned above. Readers today have access to more technology than any of their historical counterparts, and, in fact, though they would find the typewriter's keyboard familiar, they would find using it a bore. Finding out that people spent their days sitting over that machine (with no talk of carpal tunnel syndrome!) and were valued if they made no typing errors because corrections were cumbersome to make and, in some legal professions, made documents invalid, is an interesting story that involves many different aspects of history.

The desire to work is almost innate. As German socialist Ferdinand Lassalle said in the 1850s, "Workingmen we all are so far as we have the desire to make ourselves useful to human society in any way whatever." Yet each historical period offers a million different stories of the history of each job and how it was performed. And that history is the history of human society.

Each book in the Working Life series strives to tell the tale of these anonymous workers. Primary source quotes offer veracity and immediacy to each volume, letting the workers themselves tell their stories. In addition, thorough bibliographies tell students where they can find out more information and complete indexes allow for easy perusal of the text. While students learn about the work of years gone by, they gain empathy for those that toil, and, perhaps, a universal pride in taking up the work that will someday be theirs.

THE ROMANCE OF THE CAVALRY

The Civil War began at 4:30 A.M. on April 12, 1861, when artillery units of the Confederate States of America (CSA) fired on Fort Sumter in Charleston, South Carolina. This tragic conflict was fought because of important historical issues, especially slavery. Yet when young men in the North and South had to decide whether they would go to war, their reasons were personal and emotional. Northerners were angry that the eleven Southern states of the Confederacy—South Carolina, Mississippi, Florida, Alabama, Georgia, Louisiana, Texas, Virginia, Arkansas, Tennessee, and North Carolina—had split their nation in half. Southerners were furious that the United States of America was going to invade their homeland and force them to return to the Union.

William Thomas enlisted in the Ninth Pennsylvania Cavalry be-

cause, as he explains, "We had to leave home and all That was near and dear to us and go forth in defense of our country's Flag That Has been trampled in the Dust by traitors."[1] Henry Orr joined a Texas cavalry unit because he was furious that the North was trying to force Southerners to live a certain way. Orr wrote:

The storms were gathering dark over the land; we had dissolved our connection with the Federal government and declared ourselves no longer under Northern domination but a free and independent people. This enraged our northern foe, and they declared they would bring us back into the Union by suppression and subjugation, for the ties connecting us could not be dissolved. . . . The gallant sons of the South began to lay aside their domestic pursuits and prepare themselves to go forth to battle for their rights—home and fireside—and drive the invader from our soil.[2]

Many young men enlisted because of the strong passions the war created. Hatred, anger, and a thirst for vengeance blossomed after the conflict's opening battles killed thousands of soldiers. George Sargent, a bugler with the First New England Cavalry, summed up this dark emotion: "In the fall of 1861 I caught the disease called war fever, which was spreading very rapidly about that time [and that] once caught is hard to be cured, no matter how much doctoring you have done."[3]

IMAGE OF THE CAVALRY?

Once young men decided to fight, they had to select a branch of the military in which to serve. Like tens of thousands of others, all three men quoted above rode to war on the back of a horse with the cavalry. The main reason such would-be warriors chose the cavalry was that it possessed an aura of romance and glamour far greater than the infantry or artillery, a mystique that had its roots in the Middle Ages, when knights in shining armor became symbols of nobility and bravery. This ancient ideal was reinforced in America by the real-life exploits of cavalry officers like "Light-Horse" Harry Lee, a Revolutionary War hero who was still revered in the mid–nineteenth

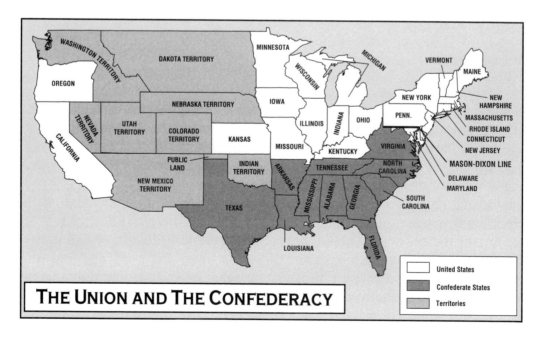

THE UNION AND THE CONFEDERACY

Many soldiers were attracted to the cavalry branch of the military because it held an aura of romance and glamour.

century for his mounted exploits to help America win its freedom.

Edward Parsons Tobie served with the First Maine Cavalry and won the Medal of Honor for his bravery in the closing days of the war. In his regimental history, Tobie explains the lure of the cavalry: "There hung about the Cavalry service a dash and excitement which attracted those men who had read and remembered the glorious achievements of "Light Horse Harry [Lee]" and of "Morgan's Men" in the Revolutionary War. Men who had read much in history and fiction preferred the Cavalry service."[4]

This romantic image was even stronger in the rural South, where most people rode horses and many young men believed fighting on horseback would be fun and adventurous. This feeling was summed up colorfully in the battle song of the

First Virginia Cavalry commanded by General James Ewell Brown (Jeb) Stuart, one of the war's best cavalry officers. The song's refrain claims:

> If you want to smell hell,
> If you want to have fun,
> If you want to catch the devil,
> Jine the cavalry.[5]

Although cavalry soldiers gloried in these words, Confederate infantry officers like General A.P. Hill hated the tune. "Keep him away—keep him away from my camp," Hill said of Stuart, who was always accompanied by a banjo player. "Every time Jeb Stuart comes around, with [Sam] Sweeney and his banjo, he makes all my division want to 'jine the cavalry.'"[6]

CAVALRY REALITY

Young recruits, however, quickly discovered that the reality of cavalry life was far different from their romantic ideals. The mobility that horses gave troopers—the military term for cavalry soldiers—enabled them to perform many tasks the infantry could not. As a result, cavalry units were busy from dawn to dusk. Troopers scouted enemy positions, served as mounted sentries called vedettes, carried messages, escorted supply wagons, and performed many other tasks.

A cavalry soldier prepares to cross a river into battle during the Civil War.

While infantry soldiers rested up for the next battle, troopers often had to ride all day and all night on various assignments. And the trooper's horse, the animal he thought would make life easy by eliminating the need to walk great distances, added to his workload because he had to spend several hours each day caring for his mount.

Henry Norton, a New York trooper, wrote after the war: "The cavalry is the hardest branch there is in the service. A cavalryman is kept busy all day long."[7] Southerners also discovered cavalry life was difficult. Henry Orr and his brother Robert fought with Parsons' Brigade, a Texas regiment. On August 21 Henry wrote from Arkansas to tell his parents that his other two brothers, James and Lafayette, had been lucky to join the infantry instead of the cavalry: "It is painful for me to be separated from them, but I am satisfied they will see better times than if they were cavalry. We have traveled a rough road since we've been in this state while all other soldiers have been lying at ease."[8]

Cavalry soldiers also quickly discovered there was little or no romance in battle, mainly because they realized they could be wounded or killed as easily as an infantry soldier. After one fierce battle, an Iowa trooper noted, "I had heard cannons fired before, but I never realized how much louder a cannon sounded when the gun was aimed toward me."[9]

REALITY OVER ROMANCE

Whether it dawned on them during long hours spent caring for their horses or in tense, frightening incidents in combat, every trooper eventually discovered the bitter reality of cavalry life. This transformation in the way troopers viewed their military service was summed up by F. Rosecrans Armie of the Second Iowa Cavalry in a letter he wrote on October 25, 1862. "I had a dim notion about the 'romance' of a soldier's life [when he enlisted]," Armie recalled. "I have bravely got over it since."[10]

The daily drudgery as well as the dangers they encountered in battle quickly made troopers realize that life in the cavalry only rarely, if ever, matched their romantic expectations about such duty. Yet troopers North and South willingly accepted these hardships; they were fighting for something they believed in so deeply that they would endure almost anything to achieve victory.

CHAPTER 1

RECRUITING AND TRAINING THE CAVALRY

During the Civil War, the United States had a military force of about 2.5 million soldiers and the Confederate States of America (CSA) had about 1.25 million. Although raising such large armies was a massive and difficult job, it was easy to recruit soldiers for the cavalry. Thousands of young men in the North eagerly responded to the dramatic appeal of newspaper advertisements like this one seeking recruits for the Tenth New York Cavalry:

> Cavalry to the Front!
> The Best Paid Arm
> of the Service!
> NO WORK IN THE
> TRENCHES!
> Three Complete Uniforms!
> LESS FATIGUE!
> LESS MORTALITY![11]

This advertisement stresses the benefits of cavalry service, even hinting it was safer than going to war on foot. But the main reason both sides found it easy to recruit cavalry was the romantic image young men held about this type of warfare. Historians claim that during the Civil War, troopers had the same heroic, glamorous image that fighter pilots have today. The romantic lure of cavalry service was even stronger in the South. North Carolina governor Henry T. Clark once complained to the Confederate War Department that "so great is the preference for cavalry that infantry [units] cannot be raised where cavalry [enlistments] can be received."[12]

UNION RECRUITING

On July 4, 1861, President Abraham Lincoln requested four hundred thousand army volunteers. By the end of the year, more than seven hundred thousand men had enlisted,

A sign in a New York City park urges citizens to volunteer for the army. Volunteers comprised the vast majority of soldiers.

including more than fifty-four thousand in the cavalry. The federal government created only a few regular army regiments, depending instead on individual states to organize the vast majority of soldiers who fought. The federal government assigned state quotas for regiments of infantry, artillery, and cavalry. Union regiments had nearly twelve hundred soldiers and officers and were identified by a number and state of origin, such as the Fourth Iowa Volunteer Cavalry. A regiment consisted of twelve companies, each with ninety-two enlisted men and three officers, and two companies made up a

squadron. A Confederate regiment was smaller, about nine hundred men, but had similarly named subdivisions.

Private citizens helped states fill military quotas. In return for recruiting and sometimes equipping a regiment, individuals could become officers. In Indiana anyone who enlisted twenty-five troopers became a lieutenant, while a person who brought in forty-five men was made a captain. People who were wealthy or influential enough to raise whole regiments became colonels and even generals.

In August 1861 James Harvey Kidd, a twenty-year-old University of Michigan freshman, recruited seventy-eight soldiers to be able to become a captain. Kidd explains how he recruited soldiers:

> The method of obtaining enlistments was to hold war meetings in schoolhouses. The recruiting officer accompanied by a good speaker would attend an evening meeting which had been duly advertised. The latter did the

talking, the former was ready with blanks to obtain signatures and administer the oath. Those meetings were generally well attended but sometimes it was difficult to induce anybody to volunteer. Once, two of us drove sixteen miles and after a fine, patriotic address of an hour, were about to return without results, when one stalwart young man

---

❧ ABSOLOM HARRISON ENLISTS ☙

The Civil War created great passions in those who fought in it. Sometimes those emotions led people to act in haste, which apparently is what happened in December 1861 to Absolom A. Harrison and his brother, Joel. Caught up in a recruiting drive, the two men from Hardin County, Kentucky, enlisted in the Fourth Kentucky to fight for the Union without consulting their wives. Absolom wrote his wife on December 12, 1861, from Camp Anderson in Jefferson County, Kentucky, to tell her what had happened and why he would not be coming home right away. In the letter Absolom comments on his worries that his family and his corn crop will not be all right. The letter is from the Internet site, www.civilwarhome.com:

Dear Wife,
I take my pen in hand to write you a few lines. I am not very well and have not been well since I left home. I have

enlisted and been sworn in. I have the promise of [becoming an officer] of some kind as soon as the regiment is organized. We have not been mustered into the United States service yet but we expect to be today or tomorrow and as soon as we are mustered in we will get our horses and uniforms. The boys from our neighborhood are all well but they are dissatisfied about not getting their uniforms sooner. Tell father to do the best he can with my corn. I have not rec'd any money yet but will get some in a few days and I will either bring or send you some. I want to come home if I can as soon as we get some money. You must do the best you can and take care of the children and if any of you get sick let me know it immediately. If I do not come home before next Thursday write and let me know how you are all getting along.

arose and announced his willingness to "jine the cavalry."[13]

Although many people like Kidd made fine officers, some who received commissions this way were failures. Regis DeTrobriand, a Union officer, wrote of one wealthy person who should have never commanded soldiers:

> I knew a retired merchant of New York who spent twenty thousand dollars to raise a regiment of cavalry in which he was, of course, commissioned colonel. His camp was near us; he was never there. He displayed his uniform on the sidewalks of Pennsylvania Avenue and in the barrooms of the great hotels. [He was] radically incapable of commanding his regiment, much less of leading it into battle.[14]

CONFEDERATE RECRUITING

In the South the recruiting effort was even harder because the newly created Confederacy did not have a standing army. The Southern effort was also more difficult because its central government—headed by President Jefferson Davis, himself a onetime Union cavalry officer—was weaker than the U.S. government and did not have much money. Thus, the South had to rely even more on individual states and private citizens to raise and equip an army.

This difficult task was made easier by the acceptance Southerners had of their need to fight and their firm belief that they would triumph. The "Charleston Mercury newspaper summed up this arrogant attitude when it bragged in its June 2, 1861, issue: "Our people are used to arms. They're accustomed to the gun and the horse. The people of the North can neither shoot a rifle nor ride a horse, unless trained."[15] The stoic spirit with which Southern volunteers accepted their fate can be seen in the attitude seventeen-year-old William Lyne Wilson had when he joined the Twelfth Virginia: "It was my fortune to exchange the books of a school-boy for the equipments of a private soldier."[16]

Cavalry regiments were raised by plantation owners and other wealthy people who donated money for uniforms, weapons, and other supplies. Although the U.S. government supplied horses to its troopers, Confederate cavalrymen had to provide their own mounts. Because of this, most troopers came from well-off families. Many Southern troopers were so wealthy that they brought along servants to take care of their horses and do chores for them.

Although the Confederate army was new, many of its officers had been trained and received battle experience courtesy of the enemy. When the war began, 144 of the 176 officers in the U.S. Cavalry were from Southern states, and most chose to fight for the Confederacy. Among the notables who switched allegiance were Robert E. Lee, who became the South's most able general, and James Ewell Brown (Jeb) Stuart, whom many historians consider the war's finest cavalry officer. Both were graduates of West Point, the U.S. Army's military college.

TRAINING CAMP PROBLEMS

When the war began, the Union had fewer than five thousand cavalry soldiers, most scattered in frontier posts from Oregon to Texas protecting settlers from Indians. By the end of 1861 more than fifty-four thousand recruits had joined the cavalry, and by war's end their ranks would swell to over 272,000. Although Southern record keeping during the war was so unreliable that no one today can know for sure, Confederate cavalry is believed to have numbered more than 137,000.

Thousands of new troopers quickly flooded into training camps that the U.S. government hastily established around the country. The First Michigan Cavalry reported to the Hamtramck Racetrack near Detroit, the

Union soldiers in a training camp pose for a photograph. The number of Union soldiers in the cavalry grew tremendously by war's end.

Eighth New York was organized at the Rochester Fairgrounds, and near Gettysburg, Pennsylvania, troopers trained in an abandoned cemetery. They were lodged in any building available, even bowling alleys, taverns, and hotels. Although many recruits endured crowded or substandard housing, J. V. Hoakison, who enlisted in the Fourth Iowa on September 5, 1861, wrote that he was first housed in a pleasant hotel: "For about three weeks [the] government paid our board and we lodged at the Brilston House [in Mount Pleasant, Iowa]. We had no guarding, no drilling or answering to roll call and soldiering was quite an easy thing from what was experienced when we were taken south [to fight]."[17]

In 1861 new troopers often had to build their training camps. This happened to the Seventh Michigan, and the amateur carpenters did such a poor job that Asa B. Ishamr remembered that the walls of their barracks "were like sieves, through which the cold air circulated freely."[18] In the winter of 1861, the First Maine was encamped in inadequate facilities at the State Fairgrounds in Augusta. Trooper Edward P. Tobie wrote that although the "weather was extremely cold, even for Maine,"[19] the regiment had no stoves for heat until November and almost the only blankets they had were for their horses. That same winter citizens in Westfield,

New York, felt so sorry for troopers at Camp Seward that they lodged many of them in their homes so they would not freeze to death.

The flood of new recruits in the war's first few months was so great that the U.S. government had trouble outfitting them, prompting President Abraham Lincoln to admit, "One of the greatest perplexities of the government is to avoid receiving troops faster than it can provide [for] them."[20] There were equipment shortages of everything from sabers to horses; some troopers trained for weeks with swords they whittled out of wood. Members of the Ninth Pennsylvania were at Camp Cameron in Harrisburg, Pennsylvania, for a week before they received their first army clothing, and that was only a pair of stockings. William Thomas of the Ninth Pennsylvania wrote home that equipment shortages and poor food had angered his fellow recruits: "It did not quite suit some of the Boys. They allowed if This is Soaldering I want to go Home again."[21]

TRAINING TROOPERS

Camps filled up with would-be troopers from every walk of life—farmers, lawyers, teachers, sailors, clerks, carpenters, newspaper reporters, bartenders, even ministers. The Fifth New York proudly boasted that its 1,065 men had previously been engaged in 126 different trades

ᒫ A LONG DAY ᒡ

The training schedule for a Union cavalry trooper was long and hard, lasting from sunrise to sunset. In Lincoln's Cavalrymen: A History of the Mounted Forces of the Army of the Potomac, 1861–1865, *Edward G. Longacre describes a typical training day. The schedule was one for the First Massachusetts Volunteer Cavalry:*

Stable call [troopers had to feed and water their horses] was blown every morning at 6:30, accompanied by sick call, followed by orderly call at 7:15 and breakfast at 7:30. Water call [for the horses] was sounded and guard mounting commenced at 8:30. The first drill of the day began at 9:30, with recall [to end it] an hour later. A second drill session began at 11:00. Recall was again blown at noon, and the men broke for dinner at 12:30. Drill resumed at 2:00 P.M.,

with recall and stable call at 3:00. Supper was eaten at 5:00. Officers received tactical instruction and the men tended to their mounts and a myriad of other chores until a quarter hour before sunset, when the regiment held retreat and dress parade. Tattoo, a lights-out call sounded at 9:00 P.M., ended the trooper's day. Every moment that the trooper was not eating, sleeping, using the latrine, doing guard duty, or exercising on the drill plain, he was attending to some other chore, usually an onerous and boring one. The maintenance and upkeep of his horse, which included a one-hour grooming session twice daily, consumed the better part of his "free" time. And if he had nothing to keep him busy in his own camp, he was often posted to guard the infantry camps.

and occupations. Turning this disorganized group of civilians into soldiers who could fight efficiently would be a long, difficult job, one that was not over when training camp ended after only a few weeks. It was believed at the time that it took two years to teach cavalry soldiers to fight effectively. Union captain Charles D. Rhodes explains why this learning process was so long and hard:

This probationary period was a wearisome one for the cavalry recruit. A trooper must perforce learn much of what his comrade of the infantry knows, and in addition must be taught all that pertains to horses and horsemanship. Those who had been fascinated by the glamour and dash of the cavalry life doubtless wished many times, during those laborious days [of training], that they had the more frequent hours of recreation granted their neighbors of the infantry.[22]

Like the infantry, the cavalry had to master the intricacies of military life, such as the proper way to salute officers and how to dress and care for their uniforms. They even had to learn how to march on foot. Cavalry soldiers often fought dismounted, and when they were off their horses, they had to march in precision ranks like infantry. In addition, troopers also had to master many intricate mounted formations that they did with other soldiers, such as riding in columns, making sweeping turns in battle, and charging the enemy.

Troopers also had to learn how to care for their horses and to use their weapons. Their basic arms were pistols, carbines (short-barreled rifles), and sabers. Although many recruits knew how to shoot, almost none of them had ever wielded a sword. Although the curved cavalry saber was so heavy that soldiers nicknamed them "wrist breakers," Thomas Crofts of the First Ohio Cavalry wrote that troopers enjoyed practicing with them: "Our first saber drill was something to be remembered. Could the hosts of rebeldom have seen the way in which we cut great gashes in the atmosphere they would have realized their cause was hopeless and would at once have given up their conflict."[23]

Cavalry soldiers were required to master various mounted formations, such as riding in columns and charging the enemy.

❧ LEARNING BY THE BOOK ❧

Much of the training cavalry troopers received came from instructional books. One of the most widely used military manuals was Cavalry Tactics: Regulations for the Instruction, Formations & Movements, the Cavalry of the Army and Volunteers of the United States *by General Philip St. George Cooke. The detailed manual covers everything from how to ride and wield a saber to instructions on how to perform mass cavalry charges.*

This is how Cooke explained the procedure for getting on a horse:

Prepare to Mount

1. At this command turn to the right, letting go the reins with the right [hand], and taking the left rein with the left hand; step two short paces to the rear, right foot leading, so as to face the saddle; at the same time, the right hand with the aid of the left, takes hold of the reins over the pommel, feeling the horse's mouth sufficiently [through the reins] to keep him steady, and then seizes also the pommel; drop the left hand by the side.

2. Insert the fore part of the left foot in the stirrup, with the aid of the left hand if necessary, and then with that hand grasp the horse's crest and mane.

Mount

At this command, spring up from the right foot in an erect posture, and instantly throw the right leg over [the horse], taking your seat gently; take the reins in the left hand, and put the right foot in the stirrup.

In his instruction on the use of the saber, Cooke warns troopers: "Great attention should at all times be paid to maintain the proper position and balance of the body; as by too great an exertion in delivering a cut or point a horseman may be thrown, or be so discomposed as to lose advantage of his skill, both for attack and defence."

This is how Cooke instructed soldiers how to make a saber stroke to the right side:

1. At the command, CUT, turn the head to the right, carry the hand near the shoulder, the point of the sabre upwards, the edge [of the sabre] to the left.

2. Extend the arm quickly to its full length, give a backhanded cut horizontally.

3. Return to the position of guard.

4. This is used against infantry, leading to the right, and cutting at the necessary angle.

Troopers were kept busy in training camp from sunrise to sundown. "Our life is a monotonous but busy round of drill, stable duty, and dress parade. . . ."[24] wrote a member of the First New England. And James R. Bowen of the Nineteenth New York complained that the eight hours of drill his company endured each day "made the men as weary as after a hard day's work in the harvest field or shop."[25]

The first training camps were often chaotic because there were not many veteran officers to teach the recruits; many newly minted officers stayed up late at night reading cavalry manuals so they could stay ahead of the men they were instructing. One trooper had this wry comment about the quality of such early training: "The blind led the blind and often both fell into the ditch, though not always at the same time."[26]

Training camp could last for several months or just a few weeks. The First New York Cavalry had one of the shortest introductions to cavalry life of any unit in the war. Formed on July 19, 1861, the recruits left training camp on July 22 and by August 1 were assigned scouting missions in Virginia.

LEARNING TO RIDE

Although one of the attractions of cavalry service had been that troopers could ride instead of walk, they usually wound up with sore feet during training camp. In addition to practicing how to march and fight while dismounted, troopers had to learn intricate riding formations on foot before attempting them on horseback. This type of training, called the "School of the Trooper,

Dismounted," was standard. However, in many cases it was also necessary because, as hard as it is to believe, many Union recruits did not know how to ride.

Historians of the Third Pennsylvania write that most of its members "had not been astride a horse until they were mustered into the [army]" and that many "showed much more fear of their horses than they ever did afterward of the enemy."[27] Captain Willard Glazier of the Second New York wrote of the trouble that troopers had learning to ride:

At first we had some exciting times with our young and untrained horses. One of the men received a kick from his horse which proved fatal to his life. . . . We find, however, that the trouble is not only with the horse, but frequently with the men, many of whom have never bridled a horse nor touched a saddle. Many [horses when first mounted] pitched up in the air as though they had suddenly been transformed into monstrous kangaroos, while the riders showed signs of having taken lessons in somersaults. [But] gradually, man and beast came to know one another.[28]

Many First Maine recruits had been sailors, and their seafaring past sometimes surfaced. One time when the regiment was parading for the Maine governor, trooper Joe Gatchell lost control of his horse. Reverting to the sailing terms he was more familiar with, Captain Prince yelled at Gatchell, "Come up there! What in hell are you falling astern for?"—to which the wayward soldier responded, "Why Captain, I can't get the damn thing in [line]!" Prince responded, "Well, give her more headway, then!"[29]

As inexperienced troopers became better riders, they had to learn more difficult skills such as riding bareback and jumping over ditches and other obstacles, often in formation with other riders. Because so many troopers fell off their horses, these drills were often chaotic.

CONFEDERATE TRAINING

In the South training was even more rushed. Troopers were needed as soon as possible because the Confederacy had gone to war with no standing army. George Cary Eggleston of the First Virginia explains:

In point of fact, they were only organized and taught the rudiments of the drill before being sent to the front as full-fledged soldiers; and it was only after a year or more of active service in

Confederate Cavalry leader Jeb Stuart in front of his troops. Stuart was known for strictly disciplining his soldiers.

the field that they began to suspect what the real work and the real character of the modern soldier is.[30]

Even though Confederate troopers often received less training, they began the war with a major advantage over their Northern adversaries — they were superior horsemen. The South was more rural than the North, which meant that its residents rode regularly, and their equestrian ability helped them dominate Union cavalry in the war's first two years. Eggleston wrote that Confederate troopers "if not actually 'born into the saddle' had climbed into it so early and lived in it so constantly that it had become the only home they knew."[31] And after viewing both armies in 1862, Garnett Joseph Wolseley, a British lord and army officer, commented:

All the [Southern] men rode well, in which particular they present a striking contrast to the Northern cavalry, who can scarcely sit on their horses, even when trotting. I have no doubt but that all who have seen Northern troopers on duty in Washington will agree with me in thinking them the greatest scarecrows under the name of cavalry that they ever saw. Every man in the South rides from childhood, and consequently is at home in the saddle;

whereas to be on horseback is a most disagreeable position for a Yankee, and one in which he rarely trusts himself.[32]

Even Union general William Tecumseh Sherman was willing to concede this superiority: "The young bloods of the South . . . war suits them, and the rascals are brave, and bold to rashness. They are splendid riders, first-rate shots, and utterly reckless—the most dangerous set of men which this war has turned loose upon the world."[33]

When First Virginia recruits arrived already adept at riding and shooting, Jeb Stuart began teaching them how to deal with the enemy. Stuart did this by leading them into situations involving contact with Union troops. Despite Stuart's relish for live action and for staying in the field for days at a time, one of his officers, Charles Blackford, said Stuart demanded the strictest discipline from his men and noted that his cavalry camp "looked like business."[34]

Training in the South was generally informal, and at times it was surrounded by an almost carnival-like atmosphere. In his war journal for November 18, 1861, Texas cavalryman Henry Orr notes that local citizens often turned out to cheer troopers during their riding drills:

During our sojourn at Camp Hebert we had very pleasant

times. We had several splendid regimental drills there which were largely attended by the citizens of the vicinity and especially the ladies who gave us smiles and would wave little flags and handkerchiefs at the soldiers, which was responded to by vociferous cheering by the soldiers.[35]

When the war began, Confederate recruits had even more equipment shortages than Union soldiers. The major problem was that the CSA did not have much money to equip its men. Although troopers brought most of their weapons from home, including shotguns, the CSA did supply cavalry with sabers. The swords, however, were often of poor quality.

❧ JEB STUART TEACHES HIS RECRUITS ❧

Confederate cavalry leader James Ewell Brown (Jeb) Stuart had a scary way of training recruits. He would lead his young cavalrymen into contact with the enemy to teach them how to handle combat situations. In A Rebel's Recollections, *First Virginia trooper George Cary Eggleston remembers the lecture Stuart gave new troopers after they had exchanged shots with Union infantry and then, at Stuart's command, leisurely ridden slowly, and not quickly, away:*

He halted us in column, with our backs to the enemy. "Attention!" he cried. "Now I want to talk to you, men. You are brave fellows, and patriotic ones too but you are ignorant of this kind of work, and I am teaching you. I want you to observe that a good man on a good horse can never be caught. Another thing: cavalry can trot away from anything, and a gallop is a gait unbecoming to a soldier, unless he is

going toward the enemy. Remember that. We gallop toward the enemy, and trot away, always. Steady now! don't break ranks!" And as the words left his lips a shell from a battery half a mile to the rear hissed over our heads. "There," he resumed. "I've been waiting for that, and watching those fellows. I knew they'd shoot too high, and I wanted you to learn how shells sound." We spent the next day or two literally within the Federal lines. We were shelled, skirmished with, charged, and surrounded scores of times, until we learned to hold in high regard our colonel's masterly skill in getting into and out of perilous positions. He seemed to blunder into them in sheer recklessness, but in getting out he showed us the quality of his genius; and before [long] we had learned, among other things, to entertain a feeling closely akin to worship for our brilliant and daring leader.

William L. Royall of the Ninth Virginia explains what happened when he tested his saber: "When I joined my company I was given a saber which I think was used in the [American] Revolution. One day [he competed] with a comrade to see which of us could cut the largest twig from a tree. I made a powerful cut and the blade of my saber broke off at the hilt."[36]

CAVALRY HORSES

When the war began, the Confederate cavalry also enjoyed another important advantage over Union troopers. They were mounted on better horses, many of them Thoroughbred racing horses from Kentucky and Virginia. Although many of the

horses were valuable, the Confederacy paid owners only forty cents a day for their use. Since Confederate troopers owned their horses, they had to buy new mounts when one was killed. This became increasingly difficult as the war went on because the South began to run out of horses. And if the cavalry soldier could not get a replacement, he would have to join the infantry—an insulting proposition to a Southern cavalryman.

But even Union cavalry were often unhappy during the war with the horses that the U.S. government bought for them. The ideal cavalry horse was young, strong, and had a lot of stamina, but troopers did not always get such fine animals. When the Ninth Pennsylvania was organ-

The Confederate Cavalry used Thoroughbred racing horses, like the one shown here. This gave them an important advantage over the Union forces.

ized, Colonel Edward C. Williams had this comment about mounts provided for his men: "A more miserable lot of horses could not again be gathered together—some were blind, lame, spavined, ring-boned [and there were even] some mares with foals. The ages of the horses varied from twenty-five years to less than three. At least a fourth, even if sound, were unfit for cavalry service."[37]

LEAVING HOME

One of the hardest experiences for new recruits was leaving behind family and friends. The Eighth New York Volunteer Cavalry from western New York State was organized at the Rochester Fairgrounds. When the regiment left Rochester, local citizens gave the newly minted troopers a joyous, though somewhat tearful send-off as they paraded through town. A story about the farewell in the November 29, 1861, edition of the *Rochester Daily Union and Advertiser* newspaper included these lines: "Among this crowd were many from the country about, friends and relatives of the volunteers who had come in to say 'Good-bye,' perhaps forever. Now and then an exchange of glances met between those in the ranks and those without, followed by an embrace, or shake of hands and not unfrequently by tears." The newspaper also reported that "one horse took fright and tore a buggy into pieces" and noted, "We hear that a boy was run over."[38] The leave-taking of Parsons' Texas Cavalry Brigade on October 13 was safer, but no less sad, when members of the unit left their camp at Bear Creek. Henry Orr explains his emotions in departing from his family:

> Truly, it was a sore trial to part with [friends and relatives], and there was scarcely a cheek that was not bathed in tears. All marched off in silence, and with my [two] brothers I went by way of [his nearby] home to bid adieu to its inmates. After eating dinner we took our leave of our Father and Mother, Sister and Brother, which was the severest trial of my life; we proceeded on our journey.[39]

Because both sides rushed troopers through training camp as quickly as possible to make them available for duty, troopers received only the bare minimum of instruction in how to operate as a cavalry unit. Many Northern soldiers, in fact, went off to war with such poor riding skills that they often fell off their horses the first time they rode into battle. It would take many months of duty, including combat in which some of them would die, for these former civilians to become veteran soldiers who truly understood how to do their jobs effectively.

CHAPTER 2

LIFE IN THE SADDLE: THE VARIED DUTIES OF THE CAVALRY TROOPER

The young men who joined the cavalry envisioned themselves as knights-errant of old, dashing off to fight in the Civil War and win everlasting glory. Although combat was only a small part of cavalry service, troopers were kept busy because their horses made them so mobile that they could perform a wide variety of duties.

The daily tasks that kept troopers in the saddle included reconnaissance —the military term for scouting enemy troops and their movements —and guard, escort, and courier duty. Cavalry jobs were arduous, boring, and often dangerous—encountering the enemy was always a possibility—and while doing these jobs, troopers became tired, dirty, and sore from long hours in the saddle, hot or cold, wet, and hungry. Charles D. Rhodes, a Union officer in the war, explains the reality of cavalry life:

After all the months of drill, how different were those days of actual service in the field—weary marches in mud, rain, and even snow; short rations for men and for horses when the [supply] trains were delayed or when there were no trains; bivouacs [sleeping] on the soggy ground with saddles for pillows; gruesome night rides when troopers threw reins on the necks of horses and slept in their saddles; nerve-wracking picket duty in contact with the foe's lines, where the whinny of a horse meant the [trooper might hear the] wicked "ping" of a hostile bullet.[40]

Confederate horsemen had just as many duties. Henry Orr wrote to his parents in Texas on August 21, 1863, from a camp on the Cache River in Arkansas about how busy his unit had been: "We have been moving and scouting continually since we left Little Rock and have had a hard road to travel."[41]

LEARNING ON THE MARCH

Like Orr, all new troopers learned that riding to war could be as tiring as marching. Bugler Cornelius Baker comments colorfully about the exhausting departure the Ninth Pennsylvania Cavalry made on January 19, 1862, from its training camp near Jeffersonville, Kentucky:

Still raining. Struck tents this morning and up to our knees in mud. Started out of Camp Andy Johnson at 9 A.M. and marched to the ferry in Jeffersonville and crossed the ferry to Louisville where we had to sit in the saddle in the streets until the whole regiment was ferried across which took till 4 P.M. Then we marched 4 miles back of Louisville and camped in a corn field in the mud and slept out in the open air. We

These weapons were all used during the Civil War. The most common sidearm used was the Colt New Model Army 1860 in .44 caliber (right).

sat in the saddle from 9 A.M. until 8 P.M. in the Evening Without Dismounting once. Our first march on Horseback. Tough one.[42]

Troopers used the term *marching* to refer to riding, and the cavalry was always marching somewhere. Troopers marched at different gaits—the speed their horses moved. At a walk, cavalry could cover four miles an hour; at a slow trot, six miles; at a maneuvering trot, eight miles; at a maneuvering gallop, twelve miles; and at an extended gallop, sixteen miles. Troopers usually rode thirty-five miles in an eight-hour day, but they could cover seventy or eighty miles in twenty-four hours.

How far they could travel and how hard they could push their horses,

ᦂ OVERLOADED CAVALRYMAN ᦂ

One of the most important lessons troopers had to learn was to carry only necessary items. The weapons, rations, clothing, and personal items they carried weighed about seventy pounds, but newcomers often doubled that load with frivolous extra items. Some troopers even bought supposedly bullet-proof jackets made of metal, but they were so uncomfortable and heavy that they soon threw them away. In his 1893 book, The Story of a Cavalry Regiment, *William Forse Scott explains that for Union troopers, "it became a fine art how to lessen the burden of their horses." His book includes the following description of an overloaded cavalryman:*

Fully equipped for the field, the green cavalryman was a fearful and wonderful object. Mounted upon his charger, in the midst of all the paraphernalia and adornments of war, a moving arsenal and military depot, he must have struck surprise, if not terror, into the minds of his enemies. Strapped and strung over his clothes, he carried a big sabre and metal scabbard four feet long, an Austrian rifle or a heavy revolver, a box of cartridges, a tin canteen for water, a haversack [cloth bag] containing rations, a tin coffee-cup, and such other devices and [items] as were recommended to his fancy as useful or beautiful. When the rider was in the saddle, begirt with all his magazine [military weapons], it was easy to imagine him, protected from any ordinary assault. His properties rose before and behind him like fortifications, and those strung over his shoulder covered well his flanks. To the uninitiated it was a mystery how the rider got into the saddle. The irreverent infantry said it was done by the aid of a derrick, or by first climbing to the top of a high fence or the fork of a tree.

and themselves, were things troopers still had to learn. Training camp had provided them with only a brief introduction to cavalry life, and every day spent in the saddle taught them new lessons about how to do their jobs. One of the most important was to carry only the essentials of war. W.W. Heartsill, a trooper with the W.P. Lane Rangers, recalls what he carried when he rode out of Marshall, Texas, in early 1861:

> Myself, saddle, bridle, saddle-blanket, curry comb, horse brush, coffee pot, tin cup, 20 lbs. ham, 200 biscuits, 5 lbs. ground coffee, 5 lbs. sugar, one large pound cake presented to me by Mrs. C.E. Talley, 6 shirts, 6 prs. socks, 3 prs. drawers, 2 prs. pants, 2 jackets, 1 pr. heavy mud boots, one Colt's revolver, one small dirk [dagger], four blankets, sixty feet of rope with a twelve inch iron pin attached [to tie horses to at night so they could graze] . . . and divers and sundry little mementos from friends.[43]

When their horses became tired from the heavy loads, Heartsill and his fellow rangers reluctantly began tossing equipment aside. Edward P. Tobie writes that First Maine troopers also "learned, by experience[,] to cast off all unnecessary impediments."[44] However, when soldiers were away from camp, they wanted more than carbines, sabers, and food; most packed a few personal items like Bibles, pictures of loved ones, and playing cards. One popular item was a "housewife," a small sewing kit with needle, thread, and buttons to repair clothes. The trick for troopers was to carry as little as possible while still having everything they needed.

RECONNAISSANCE

One of the most important cavalry jobs was scouting. The cavalry was considered the "eyes of the army" in an era in which there was no other way to track movements of opposing troops. Knowledge of where the enemy was positioned and how many soldiers there were was often the difference between winning and losing a battle, and scouting sometimes kept troopers out of camp for days at a time.

One of the most famous reconnaissance missions was "the Ride Around McClellan." From June 12 to 15, 1862, General James Ewell Brown (Jeb) Stuart led twelve hundred men in a hundred-mile circuit completely around General George B. McClellan's Union army, which was camped in Virginia. Union captain Theophilus F. Rodenbough claims the information Stuart brought back helped the Confederates defeat U.S. forces in the Battle of Cold Harbor.

General Custer and his men were almost killed when they were discovered by the Confederates while on a reconnaissance mission.

"Of most importance, he discovered the exact location of the Federal right wing, so that [General Thomas "Stonewall"] Jackson attacked it successfully,"[45] writes Rodenbough.

Scouting missions could also be short, though no less dangerous. In order to find out if Union soldiers manned a barricaded area his unit was approaching, Stuart ordered Private Jim O'Mera to expose himself to the enemy. "Ride within seventy yards of it. If the enemy is there," Stuart advised him confidently, "ride rapidly, and they will shoot behind you." O'Mera galloped along the Union line, was shot at, and his horse was wounded. O'Mera returned to calmly inform Stuart, "They're thar' yit, Ginral."[46]

Brigadier General George Armstrong Custer, known as the "Boy General" because he attained that rank at the age of twenty-three, had a similar near-fatal experience. In a letter to his sister, Ann, on March 11, 1862, Custer explained how he and his men scouted the position of Confederate artillery. After crawling on their hands and knees through dense woods to within five hundred yards of the cannons, they turned back to where they had left their horses. It was then, Custer wrote, that trouble struck: "But just as we did so the rebels discovered us and fired a shell at us. We saw the discharge and fell flat on our faces in order to avoid it. The shell passed over us and ex-ploded over our party beyond. One of the fragments struck one of our men, tearing off his arm. We allowed no grass to grow under our feet after that."[47]

GUARD, ESCORT, COURIER DUTY

A more mundane assignment was guard duty. Troopers protected mili-tary supplies; key bridges or railroad

---

◈ CAVALRY CONFUSION ◈

Almost every history written about a cav-alry regiment includes an anecdote about the chaos that resulted the first time re-cruits mounted their horses and rode out as a unit. Such was the case on December 10, 1862, when the Tenth New York Cav-alry had its first assignment—escort duty. The following account of this comical dis-aster by Captain Vanderbilt is from The Photographic History of the Civil War: Vol. 2, The Cavalry, *edited by Theo-philus F. Rodenbough:*

Please remember that my company had been mustered into the service only about six weeks before, and had received horses less than a month prior to this march. Such a rattling, jingling, jerking, scrabbling, cursing, I never heard before. Green horses—some of them had never been ridden—turned round and round, backed against each other, jumped up or stood up like trained circus-horses. Some of the boys had a pile in front on their saddles, and one in the rear, so high and heavy it took two men to saddle one horse and two men to help the fellow into his place. The horses sheered out, going sidewise, pushing the well-disposed an-imals out of position, etc. Some of the boys had never ridden anything since they galloped on a hobby horse, and they clasped their legs close together, thus unconsciously sticking the spurs into their horses' sides. Blankets slipped from under saddles and hung from one corner; saddles slipped back until they were on the rumps of horses; others turned and were on the under side of the animals; horses running and kick-ing; and all I could do was to give a hasty glance to the rear and sing out at the top of my voice, "C-l-o-s-e u-p!" But they couldn't "close [get into proper formation]."

crossings, which were vulnerable to destruction; and other key sites such as regimental headquarters. Guard duty was much more common in the Union than the Confederate army, which sought to avoid tiring its cavalry by depending on the infantry for this task.

The cavalry served as vedettes, mounted sentries who patrolled camp perimeters to prevent surprise attacks. Troopers, usually in groups of four, patrolled for up to eight hours at a time. They were often a mile or more beyond their lines, which meant they were vulnerable to attack, including assaults by sharpshooters, who fired from hundreds of yards away. Willard Glazier of the Second New York writes how miserable this job could be in bad weather:

We go out upon our shivering horses to sit in the saddle for two hours or more, facing the biting wind, and peering through the storm of sleet, snow, or rain, which unmercifully pelts us in its fury. But it were well for us if this was our worst enemy, and we consider ourselves happy if the [enemy] does not creep through the bushes impenetrable to the sight to inflict his mortal blows.[48]

The cavalry acted as guards around camps and in the field while soldiers were moving to new positions. When infantry and artillery units were themselves on the move, the cavalry ranged far ahead and to the sides in what was called screening. In this assignment, the cavalry tried to find and intercept enemy forces.

In escort duty, troopers protected high-ranking officers, payroll shipments, and wagons loaded with supplies as they moved from place to place. Accustomed to traveling quickly, the escort duty that troopers hated the most was to plod alongside wagons being pulled slowly by draft horses or mules. "Oh! deliver the cavalry from such a job as this"[49] was Willard Glazier's sarcastic reaction to a night assignment to escort wagons. First Ohio cavalryman Thomas Crofts explains why troopers hated such duty:

If you knew where you were going you never knew when you would get there. And if at a halt you sat on your horse awhile expecting it [the wagon train] to move, until both you and your horse were tired and you dismounted for a rest, it would at once move forward, and you could mount and move along at a snail's pace.[50]

Troopers served as couriers to carry dispatches, the written messages that were the army's main means of communication. Courier duty was dangerous because troopers often traveled through enemy territory. In September 1863, a week before the Battle of Chickamauga in Tennessee, Confederate trooper John Allan Wyeth had to cut through enemy lines to deliver orders to a cavalry unit near Chattanooga. Wyeth explains how he raced past a Union guard post:

> Without waiting to be halted, I tightened the reins, and crouching down close to the saddle and the horse's neck, touched him with the spurs, and he bounded forward like the wind. I saw two men leap up in front of me from the edge of the roadway. Fortunately, they did not fire. It may be that they felt something of the excitement and fright I was experiencing, but more than likely they were drowsy or asleep. In any event, in less time than it takes to tell it, I had scurried away beyond their vision and out of range of their guns.[51]

LIFE ON THE MARCH

Cavalry duties often left troopers far from the comforts of camp; when night fell they had to sleep in the wilderness. This was a new, sometimes

Two soldiers relax outside their tent at a military camp. The cavalry often acted as guards around camps and in the field.

ᴥ SWIMMING WITH HORSES ᴥ

Some of the most experienced cavalry officers in the Union and Confederate armies were soldiers from other nations. In The Union Cavalry in the Civil War, *Stephen Z. Starr explains, "It was a rare regiment of cavalry that did not have among it officers one or more veterans of a foreign army." The experience of these officers from Italy, Germany, and England proved invaluable in helping new troopers learn how to do many things. In his cavalry history, Starr quotes William L. Curry of the First Ohio, who explains how a German officer taught the regiment to swim their horses across Kentucky's Duck River:*

We had never had any experience in swimming our horses and when we started into the stream marching by fours and as the horses began to swim the fours were soon broken, and just at this time our attention was attracted by an officer [Colonel August Willich] standing on the bank shouting, "Do not break the fours." We did not know what reason there was for this, but we endeavored to keep our fours together the best we could, and soon learned that this was the only safe way to ford a stream by swimming horses, as in that manner the horses support each other and they can swim much easier and it is more safe for the men than to become scattered.

unsettling experience for soldiers like Charles C. Nott, a New York lawyer who was a captain with the Fifth Iowa. In a letter to students in New York's North Moore Street School, Nott recounts how his unit slept outside on a cold night in Kentucky:

> The men stacked their arms, and wrapped themselves in their blankets around the fires. This was my first night out. Hitherto my quarters had been in houses. I had not even passed a night in a tent. A life among the comforts of New York is not a good preparative for the field. We [he

and three others] managed to find four blankets, two of them were frozen, and a buffalo skin. The snow was scraped away from the windward side of the fire, and the two frozen blankets laid on the ground . . . the buffalo spread over the blankets. On this four of us were stretched, and very close and straight we had to lie.[52]

Nott and other troopers inexperienced in surviving in the wilderness had much to learn. The First Maine's Edward P. Tobie explains some of the lessons:

[The regiment learned] when forage is lacking, to stand by its horses, even at midnight, while they grazed [so they would not wander away]. It learned to bivouac [camp in the wild], and make itself comfortable in bivouac. On the march, it learned during a halt of five minutes to cook coffee in tin cups over a blaze of burning faggots. It learned to make three days' rations last six days. It learned also that wonderful art of kindling fires in drenching rains, in the wettest of places with the wettest of materials.[53]

FORAGING

When the cavalry left camp, troopers were given enough food to last the duration of their mission. The daily Union ration, the food a soldier consumed in one day, consisted of one pound of hard bread (called hardtack, it was so hard it was almost inedible), three-fourths of a pound of salt pork or one and a quarter pounds of fresh meat, plus sugar, coffee, and salt. However, troopers often ran out of

A soldier displays the spoils of his foraging mission. Foraging was common when soldiers were in the field longer than expected.

❧ FORAGING SOME ICE CREAM ❧

James D. Sedinger was a member of Company E of the Eighth Virginia, a unit that called itself the Border Rangers. In a diary about his wartime experiences, Sedinger fondly remembers the time in 1864 that the rangers ate ice cream, cake, and other sweets after taking them from a baker near Baltimore, Maryland. The account is from the West Virginia State Archives:

On July 10th the brigade started to burn the bridge across Gunpowder River between Baltimore and Philadelphia. Destroyed the bridge and tore up the railroad track for miles. On the evening of the 12th of July found us in the outskirts of Baltimore. The streets were barricaded, but the enemy was only militia and what a picnic we had driving them before us going almost into the heart of the city. One of the incidents of the march—the boys found a dairy filled with ice cream, cake, and everything manufactured of milk, about six miles out from the city for the city market and such a time as we had with the old German that it belonged to. Two of the Border Rangers got hold of a two gallon freezer of [ice] cream and one of the cakes. While riding along on the march eating the [ice] cream and cake, one of the Lieutenants of Company C, of the regiment said, "Hello boys, what have you to eat?" They told him. His reply was that he had the same dirt [nothing] for his breakfast. The boys tried his can and found it was Dutch cheese. The boys gave him some of theirs. He cleaned his can out and the boys divided with him. It was the first [ice] cream he had ever tasted and the first and last the company ever had during the war.

food if they were in the field longer than expected or supplies they were supposed to receive along their route were not delivered. When this happened, troopers had to find and eat whatever was available, which was called foraging. Newton A. Keen explains what the Ninth Texas ate in 1863 while traveling through Mississippi:

We lived on roasting ears [of corn] most of the time and on blackberries. One of the finest ways in the world to cook roasting ears is to build a log heap fire, and when it has burned down take your corn with shuck on, and make a large opening in the ashes, and throw in about forty or fifty ears. The only difficulty we had was in obtaining wood with which to make fire. We often used [fence] rails.[54]

Although foragers often went hungry because there was no food, they sometimes ate better than those in camp. Abner Hard, surgeon for the Eighth Illinois, said that even though the weather was cold and rainy, "the men [in the winter of 1862] preferred to stand [guard] in King George County [near Fredericksburg, Virginia], where they could forage freely, to remaining in camp and living on hard-tack and pork."[55] By foraging, they enjoyed poultry, milk, eggs, and other edibles they could not get in camp.

Although troopers tried to find food that grew naturally, they often had no choice but to eat whatever was available; sometimes they paid for it and sometimes they simply took it by force. Hungry foragers killed livestock, plucked apples off trees, and sometimes entered homes and ate food its residents had cooked. To many people, foraging seemed like theft by men armed with guns. And although every type of soldier engaged in foraging, the trooper's superior mobility made it easier for him to get what he needed, which gave the cavalry a nasty reputation at this dark art of war survival. Many Southerners even hated their own troopers for doing this. In December 1863 North Carolina governor Z.B. Vance wrote an angry letter to Confederate secretary of war J.A. Seddon in which Vance claimed:

If God Almighty had yet in store another plague worse than all others which he intended to have let loose on the Egyptians in case Pharaoh still hardened his heart [against freeing the Jews in the Bible's Old Testament], I am sure it must have been a regiment or so of half-armed, half-disciplined Confederate cavalry.[56]

CARING FOR HORSES

Troopers in the field also had to forage for their mounts. Horses required about ten pounds of grain or hay each day. It was impossible to carry those supplies on long trips, and troopers often had trouble feeding their horses, especially in areas that had been fought over repeatedly and become stripped of almost all food for men or horses. When there was no proper feed, horses munched on almost anything, as historian Douglas Southall Freeman explains: "[They] would eat the bark off trees, would gnaw through the trunks of the slender forest growth, and would devour empty bags, scraps of paper, and all the small debris of the camp."[57]

Feeding their horses was just one aspect of the troopers' most sacred duty, a task summed up by a phrase that became the credo of the cavalry —"Take care of your horse before you take care of yourself."[58] This was a serious responsibility for troopers, who depended on horses for survival;

a weak or sick horse increased the odds they could be killed. But caring for a horse was a lot of work. Union trooper William L. Curry explains how this lengthened the cavalry soldier's day almost an hour in the morning and at night:

The company must first put up the picket rope [for horses] and then the horse must be watered, fed and groomed. Then [the trooper] unsaddles, gets his coffee, and is ready to lie down an hour after the infantryman is asleep. In the morning, if the cavalry are to move at the same hour [as] the infantry they must have reveille an hour earlier than the infantry, to have time to feed, groom and saddle their horses.[59]

Caring for horses was far more complex than giving them food and water. Union Civil War captain Theophilus F. Rodenbough discusses some of the nuances of this important job:

The test of the efficient trooper was his skill in caring for his horse. When on the march a staggering animal with parched throat and fast-glazing eyes whinnied eagerly at the smell of water, it was the trooper who had to judge its proper allowance. One swallow too many for a heated horse on a long march,

multiplied by the number of troopers still ignorant of horsemanship, meant millions of dollars loss to the Union in the early stages of the war. Comparatively few horses were destroyed by wounds on the battlefield as compared with those lost through the ignorance of the troopers as to the proper methods of resting a horse, and as to the science of how, when, and what to feed him, and when to allow him to drink his fill. The southern horsemen, as a rule more experienced, needed no such training.[60]

When the war began, Union troopers' inexperience resulted in the deaths of tens of thousands of animals. Cavalry historian Stephen Z. Starr writes: "Cavalry horses were treated with a callous brutality that is almost unbelievable [and until troopers learned to care for them properly] horses were lost by the tens of thousands from overwork, exposure, inadequate food and epidemics of disease."[61]

In the first two years of the war, the Union provided 284,000 cavalry horses, even though it never had more than 60,000 troopers in the field. It is estimated that 3.5 million Union and Confederate horses died in the war, a figure that also includes horses for infantry officers and draft

The Union soldiers' poor treatment of cavalry horses resulted in the deaths of tens of thousands of animals.

horses that pulled artillery pieces and supply wagons.

PRIDE IN THEIR HORSES

Troopers generally took great pride in their horses. This was especially true for Confederate troopers who owned the horses they rode and who, at least when the war started, had superior mounts, many of them Thoroughbred racehorses. William L. Royall of the Ninth Virginia writes of the pride he had in Confederate horses:

From the foundation of the colony Virginians have been de-voted to fine horses, and in 1861 the State was as well supplied with thoroughbred and partially thoroughbred horses as with sheep and cattle. The young men in Virginia were all perfect horsemen, and mounted on their thoroughbred or half-bred horses they made a magnificent spectacle in regimental formation.[62]

Many Union troopers also admired their mounts, and they often developed deep bonds of affection for them. This is how Fifth Iowa captain Charles C. Nott lovingly described his horse:

Gipsy is one of those happy beings that everybody likes. She has never been struck with a whip or touched by the spur, and knows not what either means. The soldiers all know Gipsy, and the Germans, who are always sociably inclined, generally say as they pass her, "Good morning, Shipsy!" at which Shipsy looks as pleased as anybody could. Gipsy is small, jet black in color, and almost as delicate and agile in form as a greyhound, with the mischievous, restless eyes of a British terrier.[63]

SLEEPING IN THE SADDLE

When cavalry soldiers rode long distances or fought for days at a time, they became so tired that they often fell asleep while their horses continued to march along with the other mounts. A captain of the Second New York Cavalry explains the technique troopers used so they could sleep while riding:

Troopers learned to sleep either leaning forward on the pommel of the saddle, or on the roll of coat and blanket [behind them],

or sitting quite erect, with an occasional bow forward or to the right or left, like the swaying of a flag on a signal station, or like the careenings of a drunk man. The horse of such a sleeping man will seldom leave his place in the column, though this will sometimes occur, and the man awake at last to find himself alone with his horse which is grazing along some unknown field or woods. Some men [this way] have fallen into enemy hands.[64]

The reality of cavalry life—that it was always hard, usually boring, and sometimes dangerous—came as a shock to Union and Confederate troopers. War-minded youths on both sides of the conflict had " 'jined the cavalry" with romantic notions of riding off to war on the back of a prancing charger and winning glory in combat. But long, tiring hours in the saddle, the many tedious duties assigned them, and rough living conditions they endured in the wild all combined to kill any delusions they once had about the romance of cavalry life.

CHAPTER 3

CAVALRY RAIDERS AND GUERRILLAS

Up until the Civil War, the cavalry's main job had been to fight alongside foot soldiers in large-scale battles. But during the conflict that almost divided the nation forever, an important new role emerged for these mounted warriors. Troopers became raiders who boldly rode into enemy territory, attacking in unexpected, lightning-quick strikes that produced some of the war's most dramatic and memorable moments. In his history of the cavalry, Union officer Theophilus F. Rodenbough explains: "Cavalry operations known as raids were a distinct product of the Civil War. Both the Confederate and Federal Cavalry distinguished themselves by their endurance on their arduous and brilliant raids. The amount of destruction accomplished by this arm of the service was well-nigh incalculable."[65]

The Confederates were the first to employ this tactic. Raids, also called

"expeditions," weakened the enemy by seizing or destroying food, horses, weapons, and other military supplies; damaging key transportation facilities such as bridges and railroad lines; capturing enemy soldiers; and demoralizing and making fearful the soldiers they were fighting as well as nearby civilians.

This tactic worked so well for the South that it formed special units of Partisan Rangers, which operated independently of regular military commands to focus on raiding. These groups were called guerrillas, meaning they were engaged in irregular warfare. Guerrilla raids were mostly short excursions by small groups to destroy supplies, gather intelligence about the enemy, and harass Union soldiers in any way possible. John W. Munson, a raider under Confederate colonel John Mosby, explains that these units had complete freedom in how they operated: "Our mission was to 'annoy the enemy.' How we did it, when we did it, and where we did it, were left to our own ingenuity and application, the whole idea being to make the Federal army uncomfortable. One of our modes of annoyance was to tear up part of the railroad track and stop a train."[66]

JEB STUART'S "RIDE"

John Esten Cooke, an aide to General James Ewell Brown (Jeb) Stuart, once said that to Stuart "war seemed to be a splendid and exciting game, in which his blood coursed joyously."[67] A dandy who wore a flowing gray cloak and a feathered plume in his wide-brimmed hat, it was this sense of adventure and spontaneity that was the core of Stuart's personality and that made him one of the war's great raiders. And it was this spirit that enabled Stuart to turn a reconnaissance mission into one of the most famous of all Civil War raids.

In June 1862 General Robert E. Lee instructed Stuart to scout the army of General George McClellan, which was camped along the Chickahominy River in Virginia. In a daring raid that made him famous, Stuart brought back information about troop positions that led to a Confederate victory in the Battle of Cold Harbor and demoralized Union forces. Before dawn on Thursday, June 12, Stuart and twelve hundred troopers

headed north out of Richmond. Like other troopers, Sergeant B.J. Haden of the First Virginia Cavalry believed his unit was headed to fight Union soldiers. Instead, Stuart would lead his men entirely around the large Union army, as Haden describes: "We followed, almost at the top of our speed, thinking that at every fork of the road we would turn to the right and come out in front of the enemy; but to our surprise, at every fork, Stuart's indomitable feather [plume] was wont to bear to the left taking us directly behind the enemy's line."[68]

In the next four days, the Confederates rode in a ragged circle around McClellan's army, engaging soldiers in battle, capturing 165 prisoners, seizing 260 horses and mules, and burning and destroying tons of supplies, including one wagon intended for high-ranking officers filled with champagne and fine cigars. Stuart's men rode so swiftly that Union forces never caught them. Ironically, the cavalry that chased Stuart futilely for four days was commanded by his father-in-law, Philip St. George Cooke.

The spectacular raid was long and tiring, with Stuart and his troopers falling asleep at times in the saddle from sheer exhaustion. But the raiders were also exhilarated at what they had accomplished. In addition to damaging McClellan's forces and securing important intelligence, Stu-

Jeb Stuart's (pictured) successful raid on George McClellan's forces was the first of many Confederate raids that destroyed Union property and boosted Southern morale.

art had created a new form of warfare. Rodenbough claims that Stuart's "ride around McClellan" was "the first of the great Confederate raids that destroyed millions of dollars worth of Federal property and exercised a tremendous moral effect [that boosted Southern war spirit]."[69]

Stuart duplicated the amazing feat from October 10 to 12, 1862, when he and eighteen hundred horsemen again encircled McClellan's forces while they were camped along the upper Potomac River after the Battle of Antietam. In a raid that carried them into Maryland and Pennsylvania, Stuart's force sped through 126 miles of Union territory. The raiders briefly captured the Pennsylvania towns of Mercersburg and Chambersburg, seized twelve hundred horses, destroyed $250,000 in military supplies, damaged rail and telegraph lines, and spread fear throughout an area that had been considered safe from attack.

NATHAN BEDFORD FORREST

Stuart's raids were so successful that other Confederate officers adopted the tactic. One of the finest raiders was Brigadier General Nathan Bedford Forrest, who before the war had been a cotton grower in Tennessee and had no military background.

Forrest conducted many raids into Mississippi, Tennessee, and Alabama. In December 1862 and January 1863, Forrest was so successful at burning railroad bridges, destroying supplies, and capturing several thousand prisoners that he forced General Ulysses S. Grant to abandon his plan to invade Mississippi. Forrest was also successful in countering Union raiding forces. One of Forrest's biggest triumphs came in May 1863, when he stopped a Yankee raid into Alabama led by Colonel Abel D. Streight. Even though he was outnumbered four hundred to seventeen hundred, the brilliant cavalry tactician chased and harassed the superior Union force into submission. Forrest describes the surrender:

> I told him, "Stack your arms right along there, Colonel, and

Brigadier General Nathan Bedford Forrest (pictured) led troops on missions in Mississippi, Tennessee, and Alabama.

march your men away down into that hollow." When this was done, I ordered my men to come forward and take possession of the arms. When [Streight] saw they were barely four hundred, he demanded to have his arms back and [requested] that we should fight it out. I just laughed at him and patted him on the shoulder, and said, "Ah, Colonel, all is fair in love and war, you know."[70]

Forrest's daring raids won him the nickname the "Wizard of the Saddle" and the respect of Union general William Tecumseh Sherman. During the war Sherman referred to his foe as "that devil Forrest" but afterward called him "the most remarkable man our civil war produced."[71]

PARTISAN RANGERS

Although cavalry officers like Stuart and Forrest fought battles and performed other cavalry duties, Confederate partisan units like Captain Kirk's South Carolina Rangers and Beck's Kentucky Rangers were dedicated to raiding. The most famous raiding group was the Forty-third Battalion of Partisan Rangers, who were more commonly known as Mosby's Raiders after their leader, Colonel John Mosby.

Mosby began the war as a scout for Stuart, but in February 1863 he

Colonel John Mosby led the famous raiding group, the Forty-third Battalion of Partisan Rangers.

was given command of a ranger unit. This former Virginia lawyer had a simple philosophy that became the basis for scores of brilliantly executed raids—"A small force moving with celerity and threatening many points on a line can neutralize a hundred times its own number."[72] His men harassed Union forces in brief hit-and-run missions in which they stole supplies, burned bridges, destroyed railroad track, and attacked soldiers. Mosby's Raiders were so elusive that they were nicknamed the "Gray Ghosts of the Confederacy."

KIDNAPPING A GENERAL

One of the most brilliant Civil War achievements of any raider came the night of March 8, 1863, when John Mosby and twenty-nine others stealthily entered Fairfax Court House, Virginia, and kidnapped General Edwin H. Stoughton, who commanded Vermont's infantry. Mosby's personal account of how he captured Stoughton is from The Illustrated Confederate Reader, *edited by Rod Gragg:*

We entered the village from the direction of the railroad station. There were a few sentinels about the town, but it was so dark that they could not distinguish us from their own people. . . . We dismounted and knocked loudly at the door [where Stoughton was housed]. Soon a window above was opened, and someone asked who was there. I answered, "Fifth New York Cavalry with a dispatch for General Stoughton." The door was opened and a staff officer was before me. I took hold of his nightshirt, whispered my name in his ear, and told him to take me to General Stoughton's room. Resistance was useless, and he obeyed. A light was quickly struck, and on the bed we saw the general sleeping soundly. There was no time for ceremony, so I drew up the bedclothes, pulled up the general's shirt, and gave him a spank on his bare back, and told him to get up. He asked in an indignant tone what this meant. I told him that he was a prisoner, and that he must get up quickly and dress. I then asked him if he had ever heard of "Mosby" and he said he had. "I am Mosby," I said.

Mosby's most famous accomplishment came the night of March 8, 1863, when he and twenty-nine other Confederates sneaked into Fairfax Court House, Virginia, and kidnapped Brigadier General Edwin H. Stoughton, commander of a Vermont infantry brigade, from the comfortable home in which he slept. Mosby captured a general, two captains, thirty enlisted men, and fifty-eight horses without losing a man, a feat even he termed "an impossibility . . . one of those things a man can do only once in a lifetime."[73]

Mosby operated mainly in Virginia's Fauquier, Loudon, Fairfax, Culpeper, and Prince William Counties, an area that became known as Mosby's Confederacy. Its residents fed the rangers, sheltered them, and sometimes risked their lives to protect them from Union soldiers. Mosby's fame drew starry-eyed recruits like John W. Munson, who claimed, "To my mind Mosby was the ideal fighting man, from the tip of his plume to the rowel of his spur." Munson, a Richmond teenager of fifteen when the war began, explains the unusual existence of a Mosby ranger:

> The life led by Mosby's men was entirely different from that of any other body of soldiers during the war. His men had no camps nor fixed quarters and never slept in tents. They did not even know anything about pitching a tent. The idea of making coffee, frying bacon, or soaking hard-tack was never entertained. When we wanted to eat we stopped at a friendly farm house, or went into some little town and bought what we wanted. Every man in the command had some special farm he could call his home.[74]

Although his rangers usually operated in small groups, these guerrilla bands were so effective at raiding that the Union army had to post tens of thousands of soldiers to guard against their attacks. And that meant they were not available to fight the Confederates.

UNION RAIDERS

The Union cavalry was slower to adopt raiding, partly because the inexperience in the saddle of many troopers limited their effectiveness on such missions. Union raids differed from those of the Confederates. While Southern raiders sought to weaken and slow down an invading force, Union raids were integrated into its strategy to defeat the Confederacy. Union raids were also designed to damage civilian areas as well, because their residents and resources were helping to feed, clothe, and arm the enemy. They were also more long range, with troopers penetrating hundreds of miles into enemy territory.

The first significant Union raid came in December 1862, when more than a thousand troopers from Pennsylvania, Michigan, and Ohio traveled into east Tennessee, an area that had remained loyal to the Union but was within the Confederacy. Troopers tore up rail lines, seized horses, and destroyed anything of value. When news of the raid's success was received in Washington, D.C., General Henry W. Halleck claimed, "This expedition has proved the capacity of our cavalry for bold and dashing movements which I doubt not will be imitated by others."[75]

In mid-April 1863 General George Stoneman was sent across the Rappahannock River on a raid to Richmond, Virginia, to weaken the ability of General Robert E. Lee's army to withstand a planned invasion. Stoneman and more than forty-three hundred troopers left on April 28 and for ten days carved a wide path of destruction. Samuel L. Gracey of the Sixth Pennsylvania explains what troopers did in Columbia:

❦ RAIDS TOUGH ON HORSES ❧

Long-distance raids were hard physically on cavalry troopers, but even tougher on their horses. General George Stoneman began a raid into Virginia in April 1863 with 4,382 horses; ten days later a thousand of them were dead, injured, or so exhausted they could no longer carry soldiers. In a letter to his mother on May 12, 1863, from his camp on Potomac Creek, Captain Charles Francis Adams of the First Massachusetts comments on how horses suffered:

We were in the field four weeks, and only once did I see the enemy, even at a distance. You read of [George] Stoneman's and [Benjamin] Grierson's cavalry raids, and of the dashing celerity of their movements and their long, rapid marches. Do you know how cavalry moves? It never goes out of walk, and four miles an hour is very rapid marching, "killing to horses" as we always describe it. To cover forty miles is nearly fifteen hours march. The suffering is trifling for the men [but] with the horses it is otherwise and you have no idea of their sufferings. . . . The horse is, in active campaign, saddled on an average about fifteen hours out of the twenty four. His feed is nominally ten pounds of grain a day and, in reality, he averages about eight pounds. He has no hay and only such other feed as he can pick up during halts. The usual water he drinks is brook water, so muddy by the passage of the column as to be of the color of chocolate. Of course, sore backs are our greatest trouble. Backs soon get feverish under the saddle and the first day's march swells them; after that day by day the trouble grows. No care can stop it.

Parties were detailed to cut the canal, destroy the locks, burn the bridges, tow-boats, canal boats, etc. In ten minutes from the time we entered the town, flames were issuing from five bridges and several canal-boats loaded with forage and commissary [food] stores; another party was in town, destroying an immense storehouse filled with supplies of every description for the rebel army.[76]

Raiders also cut telegraph wires, burned wagon loads of supplies, tore up railroad lines, damaged locomotives, and captured hundreds of horses and mules. Although First Maine trooper Edward P. Tobie boasted that the raid was "the first great achievement of the Union cavalry," he admitted that the men were so exhausted when they finally returned to safety that "arguments, orders, curses loud and frequent, and even

In his letter, Adams told his mother that so many horses on both sides had died that their corpses were everywhere:

The air of Virginia is literally burdened today with the stench of dead horses, federal and confederate. You pass them on every road and find them in every field, while from their carrions you can follow the march of every army that moves. On this last raid dying horses lined the road on which Stoneman's divisions had passed, and we marched over a road made pestilent by the dead horses of the vanished rebels. Poor brutes!

A field is littered with the remains of dead horses.

blows could not keep the men awake, or the horses in their places, or scarcely any place, some of them stopping in the road sound asleep."[77]

OTHER UNION RAIDERS

As the war progressed, Union raiders became more experienced. One of the most successful strikes was in the spring of 1863, when Colonel Benjamin Grierson and a thousand men marched through Mississippi to Baton Rouge, Louisiana, where on May 2 they joined federal troops massed there. Traveling six hundred miles in sixteen days, troopers cut miles of telegraph and railroad lines, burned railroad bridges, and destroyed tons of supplies.

Just as important in the eyes of Union strategists, Union cavalry diverted Confederate troops from the defense of Vicksburg, which Grant was about to attack. As the raiders rode through Mississippi, they had to constantly fight off Confederate soldiers that followed them. Grierson and his exhausted men finally stopped to rest at a small plantation a few miles from Baton Rouge. While his troopers slept on the lawn, Grierson was invited into the plantation mansion. Afraid to fall asleep himself in case something happened that re-quired his attention, Grierson did something unusual to stay awake:

I astonished the occupants by sitting down and playing a piano which I found in the parlor, and in that manner I managed to keep awake. Only six miles then to Baton Rouge and four miles would bring us inside

---

ᦣ SPOILS OF A RAIDER ᦡ

One of the main objectives of cavalry raiders was to destroy food supplies so enemy soldiers would go hungry. Mosby's Raiders were especially good at this as they dashed behind enemy lines to intercept wagon loads of goods that they burned, although not before sampling some delicacies themselves. In Reminiscences of a Mosby Raider, *John W. Munson remembers one delicious raid in 1863:*

In the early months of the [Mosby] Command's history, the capture of a sutler [a private trader who sold army supplies] was as common as the capture of soldiers. They seemed to swarm in Fairfax County, and they traveled around without guards for, up to the time [Colonel John] Mosby went into the country, there had been no necessity for protection. On nearly all the early raids a sutler would be numbered among the spoils, and the average army sutler was not to be despised. He was a traveling retail general store with a saloon attachment, sometimes, and sometimes a bakery and confectionery to boot.

Munson describes the variety of goods taken in another raid:

I had never seen quite as interesting a collection of sutler's goods before. It was a regular bargain counter crowd, [troopers] scrambling and surging and crowding to get the best of everything. The men would eat and drink a little of everything that came within their grasp. Think of a mixture in a human stomach of sardines and raisins, cakes and claret wine, cheese, figs, beer, chocolates, pickled onions, champagne, oysters, more cheese, jelly. When every man had filled a big sack with useful things, and his stomach with what he was pleased to think "nice things," we set fire to the building and wagons and started away.

the lines guarded by the soldiers of the Union. Think of the great relief to the overtaxed mind and nerves. I felt that we had nobly accomplished the work assigned to us, and no wonder that I felt musical; who would not under like circumstances.[78]

LOOTING AND PILLAGING

The main goal of the "work" that raiders like Grierson did was to destroy anything of military value. Unfortunately, Union raiders often went beyond this accepted form of warfare and wantonly destroyed private property. They burned homes, businesses, and even churches and often stole valuables. This illegal wartime behavior is referred to as pillaging or looting, and historian Stephen Z. Starr describes such activity as "a besetting sin of the cavalry."[79]

A major factor underlying such destruction and criminal behavior was the soldiers' desire for revenge on Southerners and their belief that they had a right to do whatever they wanted to the enemy, even civilians. Cavalry on both sides of the conflict committed such illegal acts. Captain Archibald Atkinson Jr., a surgeon with the First Virginia, describes the loot raiders took from Pennsylvania stores:

One evening about 8 o'clock we reached Chambersburg, by that time the advance guard had gone up into the town & what happened there I do not know, but soon they returned with bolts of calico, silks, hats, shoes . . . and one man handed me a bolt of calico while others let the rolls fall to the grown [ground] & would ride off with the free end, saying "now boys, cut off a dress for your girl in Dixie."[80]

Union troopers had many more opportunities to loot and pillage because they spent most of the war in Confederate areas. And although officers like Major John W. Phillips of the Eighteenth Pennsylvania said, "I did all I could to stop"[81] such actions, historian Edward G. Longacre explains that this was a hopeless task: "Looting had been a way of life for many troopers since war's outset, and by mid-1864 it had become a cherished tradition. Many considered stealing one of the fringe benefits of a cavalryman's life. Others believed it was their patriotic duty to destroy the enemy's economy, one household at a time."[82]

The Union army did punish some looters. A common punishment for stealing was forty lashes with a whip, and Ninth Pennsylvania bugler Cornelius Baker witnessed the execution of a trooper from the Ninth Michigan on May 13, 1864, for looting. Though riddled with misspellings and an absence of punctuation, Baker's account is vivid: "His eyes were tied shut and

Confederate troops lay waste to a town in Maryland. Soldiers in both the North and the South looted and plllaged enemy areas.

a voly was fired and the prisner droped[.] 15 balls passed threw his body and was a instant corps[.] he was shot for killing a sitisan for his money [in North Carolina]."[83]

Troopers were especially vengeful toward the property of enemy soldiers. Samuel Gillespie of the First Ohio describes the destruction of a home near Woodstock, Virginia, owned by a Confederate colonel: "The house was deserted and the furniture destroyed. A fine piano had been chopped to pieces with an axe and the keys carried away. Fine mirrors were broken, chairs, tables and every portable thing had been carried away or wantonly destroyed."[84]

Southerners considered looting and pillaging as crimes, not acts of war. Mosby ranger W.W. Patterson tells what his unit did on August 20, 1864, when it caught up with Fifth Michigan troopers who had burned homes in Virginia's Clark County, leaving women and children without shelter:

> Orders had been passed back from our officer to "Wipe them from the face of the earth, neither asking or giving quarter," and we went at this set of howling, plundering thieves with a yell. It was a sharp, quick, and clean little fight; no prisoners. The Yankees were handicapped with all kinds of plunder. They had pillaged all the houses of every movable article before burning them, but would not allow their owners to remove anything, not even clothing, except such as they had on.[85]

Even officers were guilty of such activity. Colonel Hugh Judson Kilpatrick, who led many raids and was considered a war hero, was found guilty in 1862 of stealing two mules from a Virginia farmer and selling them. Secretary of War Edwin M. Stanton concluded after a complaint was investigated by U.S. officials, "Affidavits leave little question of [Kilpatrick's] guilt."[86] Kilpatrick, who is believed to have stolen

other articles during raids, served three months in the Old Capitol Prison in Washington, D.C. He was released on January 21, 1863, and returned to duty.

BUSHWHACKERS AND JAYHAWKERS

The cavalry's dark reputation for looting and pillaging was partially undeserved. Much of this illegal activity was committed by mounted guerrilla units that were not formally part of either army. Although such groups claimed allegiance to either the North or South, they were actually roving bands of criminals who used the war as an excuse to steal what they wanted while murdering anyone who tried to stop them.

Much of this criminal activity disguised as warfare occurred in Kansas and Missouri, border states that had been rocked by violence in the battle over slavery for a decade before the war began. Gangs from Missouri that supported the Confederacy and raided Kansas were known as Bushwhackers; their counterparts in Kansas, called Jayhawkers, brought death and destruction into Missouri.

William Clarke Quantrill was a Bushwhacker and leader of the Civil War's most savage fighting unit. A schoolteacher in Lawrence, Kansas, before the war, he formed Quantrill's Raiders. Anyone who wanted to join was asked just one question: "Will you follow orders, be true to your

❧ QUANTRILL'S RAID ON LAWRENCE ❧

The raid by William Quantrill on Lawrence, Kansas, on August 21, 1863, was one of the Civil War's bloodiest incidents. He and his guerrilla band of 450 swooped down on the unsuspecting town, killing 150 people and burning down most of its buildings. An article on the raid by Leona M. Dillard in Midwest Quarterly, *"Massacre without Tomahawks," includes an eyewitness account written in November 1888 by Mrs. M.V. Norton. This is part of what Norton experienced (the spelling and punctuation are from her original statement):*

I can only tell what I saw. It was in the morning about 4 o'clock when they came into the City—they stole in upon us without any warning. No one was prepared to receive them. Those that had their guns at home had no chance to use them—they were shot down on the instant they showed fight. I saw one man shot while his wife was holding him by the hands trying to protect him[.] they had been married about two weeks. two young Friends of ours were burned to death in a Store—after they had kindly waited upon them to everything[.] There were 14 young [army] Recruits camped on a Green or rather a Common—they were lying asleep in their Tents—all were killed. I could enumerate a great many more instances of this kind—but there would be to much sameness about it. Just imagine an Indian Massacre and you have the Quantrill Raid without the Tomahawks. . . . They took all the fine Horses there were in town—all the money—drunk all the whiskey—burned all the Houses on the principal streets. My Husband had ten cents in his Vest Pocket [after the raid] and it was all we had in the world. But we were glad to get away with our lives.

Bodies are strewn about the street in the town of Lawrence, Kansas, after Quantrill's raid.

comrades, and kill those who serve and support the Union?"[87] Although Quantrill's Raiders sometimes fought against Union cavalry units, they spent most of their time looting and destroying towns.

Quantrill's bloodiest raid came on August 21, 1863, when he led 450 men into Lawrence, Kansas, where they killed more than 150 men and boys, burned down 182 buildings, and departed with anything of value they could carry away. He and one hundred followers also showed their ruthless nature on September 10, 1863, when they raided Olathe, Kansas. J.H. Milhoan describes how some raiders guarded Olathe's men in the town square while others looted homes and businesses:

A.M. Hoff owned a store on the west side of the square, and Hoff was with the men corralled in the square. His wife, excited at the looting of the store, kept calling to her husband as she saw their property being loaded, and Mr. Hoff in his frenzy attempted to cross over where she was, when one of the guards struck him on the head with the butt end of a musket and knocked him senseless.[88]

JENNISON'S JAYHAWKERS

Although most groups such as Quantrill's were only informally aligned with the military, the Civil War's most infamous Jayhawker was a captain in the U.S. Army. When the war began, Charles Jennison formed the Seventh Kansas Cavalry, which became known as Jennison's Jayhawkers and in the first year of the war forged a record of bloodshed that rivaled anything Quantrill did.

Jennison had been a Jayhawker before the war, raiding into Missouri in the name of supporting abolition of slavery. Jennison's crimes had made him rich enough to organize a cavalry unit that terrorized Missouri. George C. Bingham, a Missourian who backed the Union, describes the destruction Jennison caused in a violent sweep through Missouri during the fall of 1861:

His entire route from Independence to Westpoint may be traced by the ruins of the dwellings of our citizens, which were first pillaged and then burned without discrimination or mercy. As they were generally constructed of wood, they are now but heaps of ashes, above which them all chimneys remain in their mute solitude.[89]

Jennison did not last long as head of the Seventh Kansas. He resigned in 1862 because the U.S. Army was going to send the regiment to fight in Mississippi and Tennessee, where it was safely removed from the temptation of looting and pillaging an area that its troopers had come to believe was their own.

MOSBY'S ORDERS

One goal of any raider was to capture enemy documents, especially those that had information on battle plans. The dispatches and letters seized, however, often concerned insignificant matters, like the letter opened once by a member of a unit led by General John Hunt Morgan, one of the South's boldest raiders.

When Morgan was told the letter was a commission that President Abraham Lincoln had signed to promote a lieutenant to captain, the famous raider decided to have some fun at the president's expense. According to a *New York Tribune* story of the time, "right under the signature of A. Lincoln, the audacious Morgan wrote 'Approved—John Morgan' and sent the commission on its way."[90]

The newspaper learned about the incident from Lincoln, who always appreciated a good joke even if it was on himself. Although the incident is humorous, it highlights the importance of raids during the Civil War. A major goal of such raids was to demoralize the enemy. Morgan's prank must surely have made Union soldiers uneasy by making them feel as if the famous raider knew everything they were doing, even which officers were being promoted.

Bold cavalry raiders who fought on both sides of the Civil War helped create a new form of combat—the raid. The mobility of their horses gave troopers the ability to strike quickly behind enemy lines in daring attacks that disrupted and demoralized their foes. It was an ingenious new concept of waging war, one that would be adopted and used extensively in future conflicts around the world.

CHAPTER 4

CAVALRY SOLDIERS IN COMBAT

When young troopers from the North and South rode off to war, they expected to fight battles that would be thrilling and adventurous. They envisioned themselves taking part in mass cavalry charges that would stir their blood and lead them to fame and glory as mounted warriors who were worthy descendants of the chivalrous armor-clad knights who hundreds of years earlier had battled evil.

But as with other aspects of cavalry life, troopers quickly became disillusioned with the reality of Civil War combat. Instead of glorious charges in major battles, most of their fighting involved small, deadly skirmishes, unimportant little engagements with the enemy that gave them few opportunities for glory but could still leave them dead or crippled from the wounds they received.

One confrontation, however, did live up to the romantic expectations of war that troopers from both sides had held. It was the Battle of Brandy Station.

On June 9, 1863, the largest, most dramatic cavalry battle that ever took place in North America raged for over ten hours at Brandy Station, a tiny community thirty-five miles southeast of Fredericksburg, Virginia. Of the twenty thousand soldiers who fought that day, about seventeen thousand were cavalry. Major General James Ewell Brown (Jeb) Stuart commanded ninety-five hundred cavalry and some artillery, while Brigadier General Alfred Pleasonton led eight thousand troopers and about three thousand infantrymen.

Sergeant William F. Moyer of the First Pennsylvania eloquently describes how the two sides joined in battle:

In an instant, a thousand glittering sabres flashed in the sunlight, and from a thousand brave and confident spirits arose a shout of defiance which, caught up by rank after rank, formed one vast, strong, full-volumed battle-cry, and every trooper rising in his stirrups dashed headlong at the foe. First came the dead, heavy crash of the meeting columns, and next the clash of sabre and the rattle of pistol and carbine, mingled with frenzied imprecations; wild shrieks that followed the death blow . . . forming the horrid din of battle. For a few brief moments the enemy stood and bravely fought, and hand to hand, face to face, raged the contest; but, quailing at length before the relentless force of our attack and shrinking from the savage gleam and murderous stroke of our swift descending sabres, they at length broke and fled in confusion.[91]

The bold cavalry charges, massed counterattacks, and nonstop fighting that continued throughout the long and bloody day made the Battle of Brandy Station the Civil War's most storied clash of cavalry. The fight was also important because it was

Union cavalry charge at Confederate troops at the Battle of Brandy Station. Unlike the small skirmishes that comprised most of the fighting of the Civil War, Brandy Station was a full-scale battle.

the first in a series of engagements that led to the war's most famous battle, at Gettysburg, Pennsylvania, from July 1 to 3, when the Union turned back an invasion force led by General Robert E. Lee.

For troopers on both sides, Brandy Station brought to life all the fanciful notions about mounted warfare that had led them to join the cavalry. Captain William Blackford, a member of Stuart's staff, wrote that it was

> a passage of arms filled with romantic interest and splendor to a degree unequaled by anything our war produced. It was like what we read of in the days of chivalry, acres and acres of horsemen, sparkling with sabers and brilliant bit of color where their flags danced about them, hurled against each other at full speed and meeting with a shock that made the earth tremble.[92]

This dramatic, historic battle, however, was an aberration in how troopers normally fought. Cavalry combat usually consisted of smaller, far less glorious clashes with the enemy. Mass cavalry charges were rarely used, and during some fights troopers were not even riding horses.

HOW THEY FOUGHT

When the war began, Union and Confederate cavalry tactics were patterned after those used in European wars. Although these strategies relied on mass assaults by saber-wielding horsemen, several factors made them ineffective in most Civil War battles.

One important factor was that the terrain of most battle sites was unsuited to cavalry charges. They had too many trees, rocks, streams, and hills, obstacles that slowed down onrushing cavalrymen and caused the charge to falter and break apart. A second factor was that although charges worked well when cavalry faced cavalry, they were often suicidal against infantry units armed with more powerful weapons than European soldiers had. Historian James M. Merrill explains: "The increased range of rifles and the invention of guns [that were loaded with multiple bullets], making continuous long-range fire possible, destroyed the effectiveness of saber-charging horsemen against trained infantry."[93]

In Europe, the weapons that foot soldiers carried were not accurate beyond a hundred yards. But Civil War rifles could accurately fire a minié ball (lead bullet) four or five times that far. The greater range, stopping power, and accuracy of these more powerful weapons meant that infantry could kill many more charging cavalrymen before the onrushing horsemen could engage them in combat.

As a result of these factors, the two sides began to use cavalry in

࣭ FIRST TIME IN COMBAT ࣭

A soldier's first time in combat was memorable, an experience he would never forget. In The Illustrated Confederate Reader, *editor Rod Gragg includes a letter that Kentucky cavalryman John H. Hines wrote home April 22, 1862, about the sounds and sights of the Battle of Shiloh:*

For three miles in one unbroken line stood our troops, their fixed bayonets glistening in the new sunbeams, for the sun was just coming over the top of a small elevation. Almost every hill now on both sides looked like a volcano, for the deep mouthed cannon were roaring on every side. Soon the rattle of musketry announced that our vanguard had found the foe. Being mounted and ordered to different places during the day, I had an opportunity to see everything that happened almost. I can assure you that a battlefield is far from being a pleasant place, laying aside the dangers of being hurt, because you can't get out of hearing the groans of the dying or out of sight of the death.

For many, the most important thing about their first fight was how they reacted to danger. In Sketches of War: Letters to the North Moore Street School of New York, *Captain Charles C. Nott of the Fifth Iowa explains that he was amazed at his lack of fear:*

You will perhaps ask how I felt. There was nothing upon which I had had so much curiosity as to what my feelings would be. Much to my surprise I found myself pleasantly cool. I did not get excited, and felt a great want of something to do. There seemed such a certainty of being hit that I felt certain I should be, and after a few minutes had a vague sort of wish that it would come if it were coming and be over with. Take it altogether, I think I felt and acted pretty much as I do in any unusual and exciting affair.

new ways in combat. One innovation was to have troopers dismount and fight, in effect making them mobile infantrymen. Historian Gregory J. Urwin explains:

The Civil War allowed the United States Cavalry to shake off outmoded European notions [about tactics] and adopt a more pragmatic and thoroughly American doctrine. Romantics like [Union general] George A. Custer still practiced the saber charge with great effect, but even he accepted the new conception of mounted warfare. Cavalrymen were no longer shock troops, but highly mobile gunmen who could use their horses to deny strategic positions to the enemy and hold them with rapid-fire repeating carbines until infantry support arrived.[94]

The new strategy made troopers more versatile fighters. And combined with their new task of raiding behind enemy lines, they had many more opportunities to fight the enemy, although usually not in full-scale battles. But as their combat role changed, so did the way troopers used their weapons.

WEAPONS

When the war began, James H. Stevenson of the First New York wrote, "A swift horse, a good pair of spurs, and a sharp saber are the chief weapons of a trooper. Pistols and carbines are but incidentals."[95] Although cavalrymen at first delighted in the romance of carrying and

This collection of Civil War weapons includes one 58-caliber musket (top) and four different types of carbine rifles.

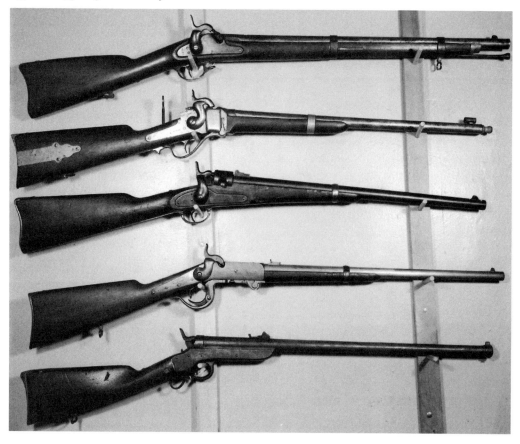

wielding sabers, they were not that important in battle; records show that in four years of combat, Union hospitals treated fewer than a thousand saber wounds.

The weapons Union troopers relied on were pistols and carbines, lightweight rifles almost twenty inches shorter than the fifty-six-inch long infantry muskets and easier to handle on horseback. And by 1863 the Union had new carbines like the Sharp's, which held multiple bullets to allow continuous fire. Most Confederate and Union infantry had muzzle-loaders, rifles that had to be slowly loaded by pouring gunpowder down the barrel and then ramming

home a chunk of lead to fire just one shot.

The increased firepower that carbines gave troopers amazed Confederate soldiers, who joked that Union troopers could load them on Monday and shoot them all week. Trooper Franklin H. Bailey of the Fourth Michigan wrote in March 1865 that some rebels surrendered just to see the magical Yankee guns: "The rebs that we took while on a scout from Rossville said they dreaded to come across our bridge, for we kept shooting all of the time. When they see our guns they say 'No wonder *yourns* shoot so fast. If *weuns* had such guns we'd fight longer.'"[96]

⚔ CAVALRY HORSES IN BATTLE ⚔

Troopers often developed loving relationships with their horses, a bond that was never stronger than in battle. In Clash of Cavalry: The Battle of Brandy Station, June 9, 1863, *Fairfax Downey includes the words of praise New York trooper Elmer Eugene Barker wrote about warhorses:*

[Veteran horses] seemed to share the hopes and fears of battle equally with their riders. When sabres were drawn and the troops cheered, the horses gallantly responded. If a volley came in a charge and the horse was unhurt, he would lower his head and toss it from side to side. In charging infantry, he would charge straight at a man and knock him down; if against cavalry, he would lift his head and forefeet as though going over a fence. . . . A horse, even with a foot shot off, would not drop. He might be fatally wounded but he would hobble on or stand with drooping head until loss of blood brought him down. They became attached to their riders and to one another and kept their places in the ranks, even when riderless. If one lost his rider and was not wounded, he continued galloping here and there, neighing with fear and alarm, but would not leave the field.

Many of those carbines did get into rebel hands when raiders captured them. As the war progressed and the Confederacy had trouble supplying soldiers with even basic items such as uniforms, Southerners began relying so much on what they could steal from the enemy that a Virginia trooper joked, "Everything but ourselves was branded U.S."[97]

Although Southern troopers carried carbines, most of them capable of firing only one shot at a time, they relied more on other weapons than Union soldiers. A Confederate favorite was the twelve-gauge shotgun, and almost every trooper carried a large knife, which they used with greater ease than swords. Samuel B. Barron of the Third Texas wrote of how much troopers admired such weapons: "A large number had huge knives made in the blacksmith shops, with blades eighteen to twenty-four inches long, shaped something like a butcher's cleaver . . . and with these deadly weapons the boys expected to ride through the ranks of the Federal armies and chop down the enemy right and left."[98]

Mosby's Raiders preferred fighting with a pair of forty-four-caliber revolvers; some carried as many as four at one time. John W. Munson recalls how raiders wielded them in their brief, often deadly encounters with Union soldiers: "Long and frequent practice had made every man in the Command a good shot and each was as sure of his revolver as every cowboy is with his six-shooter. As a general thing our real fights were fast and furious and quickly over, one or the other side withdrawing at a dead run when the pistols were empty."[99]

UNEXPECTED MEETINGS

The brief but deadly fights Munson describes were typical of cavalry combat. Although massive battles like Gettysburg and Chickamauga are featured in history books, the Civil War had over ten thousand separate military actions, most minor skirmishes involving a few soldiers. And whether cavalrymen were on a raid, scouting, standing guard, or escorting a wagon train, the potential for combat always existed.

While scouting on August 3, 1863, in Arkansas, the First Wisconsin was camped for the night at Hodges Ferry on the L'Anguile River. Suddenly they were attacked by Texas cavalrymen. "Our first alarm," wrote Lieutenant John A. Owens, one of twenty troopers to escape, "was the frightened shrieks of the negroes [camp helpers] and the yells of the Rebels. For 20 minutes the unequal contest raged, till 50 of our men were killed and wounded and an equal number of Rebels lay dead and dying on the ground."[100]

William L. Royall of the Ninth Virginia was also unexpectedly thrust

❧ THE SIXTH PENNSYLVANIA LANCERS ❧

Although it is hard to believe, one Civil War cavalry regiment was armed with lances. Inspired by similarly equipped European units, General George McClellan ordered the Sixth Pennsylvania to be armed with nine-foot-long spears when it was organized in December 1861. Named Rush's Lancers after Colonel Richard H. Rush, the experiment failed miserably. Lances were a poor weapon against soldiers armed with rifles, and by May 1863 the Sixth Pennsylvania traded its lances for carbines. One fight that proved lances did not work came near Richmond, Virginia, on June 27, 1863, when Rush's Lancers faced First Virginia troopers. This description of the confrontation by Confederate officer W.W. Blackford is from The Union Cavalry in the Civil War *by Stephen Z. Starr:*

I felt a little creeping of the flesh when I saw this splendid looking body of men, about seven hundred strong, drawn up in line for battle in a large open field two or three hundred yards off, armed with long poles with glittering steel points. The appearance they presented was certainly very fine, with a tall forest of lances held erect, and at the end of each, just below the head, a red pennant fluttering in the breeze. [Stuart] quickly threw a regiment into line and ordered the charge [and] down upon them we swept with a yell, at full speed. They lowered their lances to a level and started in fine style to meet us midway, but long before we reached them the gay lancers' hearts failed them and they turned to fly. For miles the exciting chase was kept up, the road was strewn with lances thrown away in their flight, and nothing but the fleetness of their horses saved them all from capture.

The Sixth Pennsylvania Cavalry, also known as Rush's Lancers, pose for a photograph.

into combat. While riding with several comrades, Royall came unexpectedly on two Union soldiers and he killed one of them. Royall describes the encounter:

> In turning a corner in some very thick pines we came face to face with two mounted Federal soldiers not twenty feet from us. I called out at once to them, "Surrender!" Instead of doing so the man on my side of the road commenced drawing his revolver. I raised my carbine to my shoulder and . . . I made the luckiest of shots. I struck him at the pit of his right arm and cut it almost off. His cocked revolver fell from his hand. It was at full cock and in another instant he would have fired.[101]

Cavalry units clashed frequently because both sides roamed freely through enemy territory. And although troopers could be killed in such encounters, they seemed to relish the adventure of such brushes with the enemy. Lieutenant Theodore Stanford Garrett Jr., who enlisted in the First Virginia when he was only fifteen, recalls with excitement a skirmish with Union soldiers in late November 1863 near Fredericksburg:

> Bang! Bang!—the smoke rises all around [us], and Whiz! Thud! there goes Archie's (my messmate's) horse down on his nose, and his rider playing leapfrog over his head. Zip!—a ball hits the pommel of my saddle, and I rein my horse in [and] blaze away into the thick crowd of men and horses standing there, bringing down only two or three [although] it seemed to be almost impossible to shoot into such a crowd without hitting something. And yet I ask any unprejudiced person if it isn't a very difficult matter to hit the side of a barn if you are in momentary apprehension that the aforesaid barn is going to return the compliment.[102]

An added irony to these unexpected encounters was that occasionally Confederate officers ran into Union troops they had once commanded. Captain James McIntosh resigned from the U.S. Cavalry on May 17, 1861, to fight for his native Florida. Nearly three months later, he faced his former company at Dug Spring, Missouri. "My god, boys, that's Captain McIntosh,"[103] exclaimed one Union trooper. The soldiers he once led fired over his head so he could escape unharmed, and as McIntosh rode away he doffed his hat to them.

FIGHTING IN BIG BATTLES
Although most combat occurred in minor engagements, troopers played

a significant role in some major battles, even though they were far outnumbered by foot soldiers. And the cavalry charge was often their most important contribution to victory.

The most famous early charge occurred in the war's first major battle, at Bull Run on July 21, 1861. Stuart led the First Virginia into the fight, charging a column of New York Zouaves. The infantry soldiers panicked and as they fled screamed, "The Black Horse Cavalry are coming!"[104] —a reference to the regiment's pref-

erence for black horses. Although Union forces were already slowly being beaten back by Confederate infantry, Stuart's troopers helped turn it into a full-scale retreat.

Stuart's glorious charge was no fluke. The Confederate cavalry was a powerful force early in the war and dominated Union horsemen whenever they met. But as Northern troopers acquired the skills and experience to fight, they began to have their own moments of honor. One came on September 19, 1864, during the Bat-

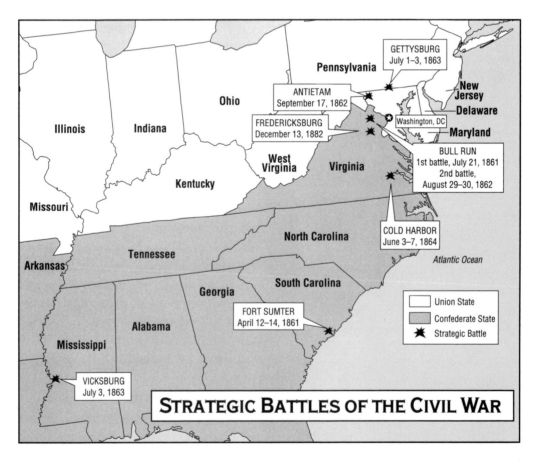

STRATEGIC BATTLES OF THE CIVIL WAR

❦ CAVALRY CHARGE GONE AWRY ❧

A cavalry charge could be a thing of terrifying beauty, but one that failed was a living nightmare for any trooper involved. In The History of the First New Jersey Cavalry, *regimental chaplain Henry R. Pyne explains how a charge on June 6, 1863, against Confederate infantry near Harrisonburg, Virginia, turned disastrous when infantry fire turned back the massed cavalry assault. Pyne's vivid description is from* Lincoln's Cavalrymen: A History of the Mounted Forces of the Army of the Potomac, 1861–1865, *by Edward G. Longacre:*

If a cavalry charge is glorious, a cavalry rout is dreadful. Pressing upon one another, straining to the utmost of their speed, the horses catch an infection of fear which rouses them to frenzy. The men, losing their places in the ranks, and all power of formation or hope of combined resistance, rush madly for some point of safety upon which it may be possible to rally. Each check [halt] in front makes the mass behind more dense and desperate, until horse and men are overthrown and ridden over, trampled on by others as helpless as themselves to rescue or to spare. The speed grows momentarily faster. Splashing through the pools of mire, breaking down fences, darting under trees, with clang of sabres and din of hoofs, officers wild with shame and rage, shouting themselves hoarse with unavailing curses, and the bullets of the enemy whistling shrilly overhead, the mingled mass sweeps on, until utter exhaustion stops [them].

Pyne ends his account by explaining that the maddened men and horses finally escaped from "the field of their defeat, leaving their colonel, three captains, one-twelfth of their troopers, and the regimental colors in the hands of the enemy.

tle of Opequon Creek, when Union infantry and cavalry defeated the Confederates near Winchester, Virginia. A stirring charge against barricaded infantry in that battle is described by Lieutenant William H. Harrison of the Second U.S. Cavalry:

At the sound of the bugle we took the trot, the gallop, and then the charge. As we neared their line we were welcomed by a fearful musketry fire, which temporarily confused the leading squadron [but] instantly, officers cried out, "Forward! Forward!" In a moment we were face to face with the enemy. They stood as if awed by the heroism of our brigade, and in an instant broke in complete rout, our men sabering them as they vainly sought safety in flight.[105]

Infantrymen lie dead on the Gettysburg battlefield. Due to their large numbers, many more infantry soldiers were killed during the Civil War than cavalrymen.

Cavalry charges were not a significant factor in many major battles. In fact, troopers sometimes fought in a way they had never expected when they enlisted—on foot. As the war progressed, cavalry officers for both sides began to use dismounted troopers for a variety of reasons—to seize and hold ground until infantry arrived, fill gaps in lines of battle, cover the retreat of infantry, or simply fight where the ground was impractical for mounted warfare. An example of this occurred during the Battle of Gettysburg, July 1–3, 1863, when

Eighth Illinois lieutenant Amasa Dana dismounted his men to hold back infantry, as he remembers:

I could see the enemy skirmish line reaching from left to right for a distance of a mile and a half. Dismounting my entire company and sending the horses to the rear I formed the first line of twenty men including myself. The enemy advanced slowly and cautiously. Our first position proved to be well taken. In front there was a large open field.

Scattering my men to the left and right at intervals of thirty feet and behind posts and rail fences I directed them to throw their carbines sights up for 800 yards. We gave the enemy the benefit of long range practice. The firing was rapid from our carbines, and induced the belief of four times the number actually present.[106]

DEAD CAVALRYMEN?

Although cavalry on both sides fought bravely and often in major battles as well as skirmishes, many more infantry soldiers than troopers were killed. This was mainly due to the fact that there were many more infantry soldiers than cavalry, and partly because troopers did not always fight in major battles, either due to unfavorable terrain or the nature of the battle. This discrepancy once led Major General Joseph Hooker, an infantryman who commanded the Union's main army early in the war, to mockingly claim, "No one ever saw a dead cavalrymen."[107]

While there are no reliable statistics on how many cavalrymen were killed in battle, thousands of troopers gave their lives. Stuart defended

After the Battle of Antietam, Stuart praised his troops for the sacrifices they made during battle, even though they had not lost as many men as the infantry.

his men against such taunts as Hooker's after the Battle of Antietam on September 17, 1862, when the Union halted the Confederate invasion of Maryland. Although Stuart admitted his cavalry had not lost as many men as the infantry, he praised the sacrifices they had made:

> My command did not suffer on any one day as much as their comrades of other arms, but there was the sleepless watch and the harassing daily "petite guerre [small battles] in which the aggregates of casualties sums up heavily. There was not a single day, from the time my command crossed the Potomac [River] until it recrossed it that I was not engaged with the enemy. Their services were indispensable to every success obtained.[108]

Stuart's defense assumed added meaning with his own death a day after being wounded May 11, 1864, in the Battle of Yellow Tavern while leading his men against Union cavalry thrusting toward Richmond, Virginia. Stuart was on the front line when a Michigan trooper shot him. Major H.B. McClellan, an aide to Stuart, described his death in a letter to Stuart's widow:

> One man, who had been dismounted in the charge and was running out on foot, turned, as he passed the General, and, discharging his pistol, inflicted the fatal wound. As he was being brought off [the battlefield], he spoke to our men, whom he saw retreating, and said: "Go back! go back! and do your duty as I have done mine, and our country will be safe. Go back! go back! I had rather die than be whipped."[109]

Death could come to soldiers quickly, unexpectedly, and often capriciously, taking one life while sparing another. Ninth Tennessee trooper John Weatherred wrote in his diary how a friend died while fighting next to him: "Jack Carter, to my left by 4 feet, rose on his knee and said I'll get that yank behind that tree and fired, but Jack fell dead, shot through the head."[110] William Thomas of the Ninth Pennsylvania explains how a soldier sleeping beside him was killed the night of July 6, 1862:

> We were surprised in camp this morning about 2 o'clock A.M. by a party of Guerillas[.] They came up behind the camp and shot down the gaurd and then fired into the tents[.] Our tent is riddled with balls[.] Henry Feindt who was sleeping by my side Had a Ball to graze the top of His head[.] The guerillas then fled into the woods and made their escape[.][111]

And many troopers died in cavalry charges, which did not always end in glory. At the Battle of Gettysburg on July 3, 1863, General Hugh Judson Kilpatrick ordered the First Vermont to charge Texas and Arkansas infantry, which were well protected by earthen barricades. Several cavalry regiments had already suffered huge losses in failed attempts to dislodge the infantry from its protected spot.

But Kilpatrick, nicknamed "Kill Cavalry" by his own men because of his reckless disregard for their lives, ordered another attack because he wanted the glory of defeating them.

"General, do you mean it? Shall I throw my handful of men over rough ground, through timber, against a brigade of infantry?" [112] asked First Vermont general Elon Farnsworth. Kilpatrick would not relent, and as

⚔ NOT EASY TO CHARGE ⚔

In July 1861 Captain William W. Blackford, an aide to General James Ewell Brown (Jeb) Stuart, found out how difficult it was to take part in a cavalry charge. The following account of his problems handling his horse, Comet, during the First Battle of Bull Run is from The Illustrated Confederate Reader, *edited by Rod Gragg:*

While a Lieutenant in my company, I had carried a Sharp's carbine slung to my shoulder and this I still wore; I also had my saber and a large sized five-shooter [revolver]. In the occupation of the moment I had not thought which of my weapons to draw until I had started, and as it does not take long for a horse at full speed to pass over seventy yards, I had little time to make the selection. I found, in fact, that it would be impossible to get to either my saber or pistol in time, and as

the carbine hung conveniently under my right hand I seized and cocked that, holding it in my right hand with my thumb on the hammer and finger on the trigger. I thought I would fire it and then use it for a crushing blow, in which it would be almost as effective against a man standing on the ground as a saber. The tremendous impetus of horses at full speed broke through and scattered their line like chaff before the wind. I then plunged my spurs into Comet's flanks and he [soon knocked over an enemy soldier]. I leaped down from the saddle, rammed the muzzle of the carbine into the stomach of my man and pulled the trigger. I could not help feeling a little sorry for the fellow as he lifted his handsome face to mine while he tried to get his bayonet up to meet me; but he was too slow, for the carbine blew a hole as big as my arm clear through him.

the Vermonters prepared to charge, one trooper remembered years later that "each man felt, as he tightened his belt, that he was summoned at a ride to death."[113] The charge over an area littered with trees, rocks, and streams proved suicidal; sixty-five of the three hundred troopers were killed or captured, and Farnsworth was one of the fatalities.

BRANDY STATION

Many cavalrymen died after the Battle of Brandy Station. The Union suffered 866 casualties (men who were killed, wounded, or captured) and the Confederate total was 575. The battle occurred because Hooker had learned that Stuart's cavalry was massing at Brandy Station. Fearing the damage Stuart could do in a raid, Hooker decided to attack him first to weaken him.

The daylong battle began about 4:30 A.M. when Brigadier General John Buford crossed the Rappahannock River and surprised the Confederates at Beverly's Ford. Caught

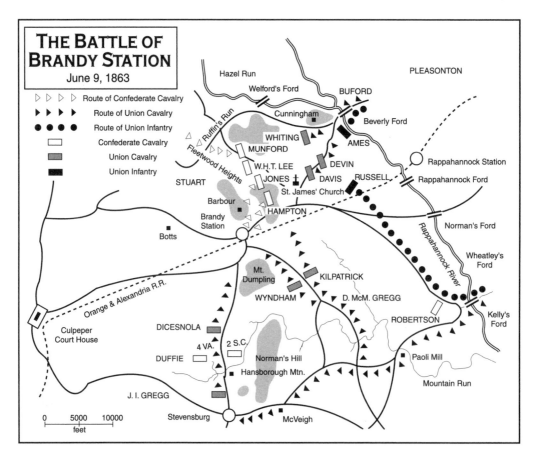

THE BATTLE OF BRANDY STATION
June 9, 1863

▷ ▷ ▷ ▷ Route of Confederate Cavalry
▶ ▶ ▶ ▶ Route of Union Cavalry
● ● ● ● Route of Union Infantry
☐ Confederate Cavalry
▨ Union Cavalry
■ Union Infantry

Union and Confederate troops engage in hand-to-hand combat. The prospect of charging into columns of armed men could instill fear in even the bravest of soldiers.

by surprise, Stuart gathered his forces and the nearly twenty thousand soldiers fought for the next ten hours. Cavalry units charged one another repeatedly and engaged in running skirmishes for hours in a giant battle that swirled for miles around Brandy Station.

When the Union cavalry finally broke off the fighting that afternoon, the bodies of soldiers and horses lit-tered the plain. Union captain Charles D. Rhodes writes that the ferocity with which soldiers fought that day was evident even after they had died: "In this terrible cavalry combat every possible weapon was utilized, and after it was over, men were found interlocked in each other's arms, with fingers so firmly imbedded in the flesh as to require force to remove them."[114]

Although U.S. troopers had left the field to the Confederates, Brandy Station was considered a major and historic victory for Union cavalry. For the first two years of the war, Union mounted forces had never prevailed in any encounter larger than a minor skirmish. Brandy Station was not only the Union's first significant cavalry victory; it signaled there were many more to come. Major McClellan of Stuart's staff admitted: "One result of incalculable importance certainly did follow this battle—it *made* the Federal cavalry. Up to that time confessedly inferior to the Southern horsemen, they gained on this day that confidence in themselves and in their commanders which enabled them to contest so fiercely [in the rest of the war]."[115]

ON BEING AFRAID

Going into combat, every trooper knew he could be killed or wounded. Combat was frightening, and after one battle George Sargent of the First New England wrote that fear was an emotion every soldier knew:

Presently we got the order to get ready to charge. Can you imagine a fellow's feelings about that time, to have to face thousands of muskets with a prospect of having a bullet put through you? I've heard some say that they were not scared on going into a fight, but I think it's all nonsense. I don't believe there was ever a man who went into battle but what was scared, more or less. Some will turn pale as a sheet, look wild and ferocious, some will be so excited that they don't know what they are about while others will be as cool and collected as on other occasions.[116]

As Sargent notes, fear was an emotion troopers had to deal with throughout the war; even men who won medals and were considered brave were afraid. But somehow troopers on both sides of this deadly conflict, as have soldiers in every era before and since then, learned to overcome their fears and to fight and die for their respective countries.

CHAPTER 5

NONCOMBAT LIFE OF THE CAVALRY

Long hours in the saddle and harsh conditions in the field made Union and Confederate troopers appreciate the quiet times when they were not on duty. After weeks of scouting and skirmishing with enemy troops, George Sargent, a bugler for the First New Hampshire, wrote in his diary for September 21, 1862, how good it was to relax at a camp near Poolesville, Maryland:

> We arrived here ragged and dirty after a long campaign. We went into camp in a pleasant grove just outside of the town. We enjoyed ourselves here hugely: nothing to do but play [music], take care of our horses, and cook our grub. Our rations were good and plenty of them, fresh beef, salt pork, potatoes, beans, dried apple, soft bread, coffee and sugar. We had the fa-vorite New England dish, baked beans, every few days. [117]

Sergeant Henry G. Orr of the Twelfth Texas had the same feeling of almost blissful contentment while members of Parsons' Brigade rested at Camp Hope on the Cache River in Arkansas. In a letter to his parents dated August 21, 1863, Orr wrote: "This is by far the best and most pleasant campground we have ever found. We have wells of splendid water and both regiments cannot exhaust [it]. We also get plenty of corn for our horses. There are no Feds [Union soldiers] near here now." [118]

For both Orr and Sargent, perhaps the best thing about camp life was being safe from enemy attack. But they could also sleep in tents or wooden barracks instead of out in the open, see a doctor, and enjoy the camaraderie of other soldiers.

HAVING FUN

Troopers greatly enjoyed being in camp because they could relax there and forget about the war. Randolph Harrison McKim, a chaplain in the Second Virginia, describes their quiet time at night:

> Wouldn't you like to peep in on us some evening as we sit [in tents] around our stove amusing ourselves until it is time to retire? We are a happy but a boisterous family. Our amusements are various—reading, singing, and writing. We employ the twilight in conversation, the subject of which is the "latest grapevine" (i.e., rumor), or a joke on the Colonel, or when we are alone, our do-

Soldiers perform mock combat exercises. Camp gave troopers the opportunity to relax and amuse themselves while resting from the war for a short time.

mestic concerns. As soon as night sets in the candles are lit and we draw round the stove and take down our book, or else someone reads aloud.[119]

Like young men in any era, troopers liked to compete against one another. They played horseshoes, checkers, and engaged in athletic contests, including a new game more popular in the South than the North. Known by various names including townball, the sport was an early form of baseball. In his diary for December 21, 1861, Henry Orr describes a game at Camp Hebert in Texas: "The boys have several ways of amusing themselves; the most popular at present is townball. Each company has some two or three indian rubber balls, and they choose about ten or fifteen from each side. Such knocking, running, and shouting was never heard. The captains and lieutenants sometimes take a hand."[120]

Union soldiers also played baseball. One game on Christmas Day 1862 between squads from various teams was watched by an estimated forty thousand spectators, a crowd that is believed to have been the largest to witness any sporting event in the nineteenth century.

Some competitions were just for fun, like the snowball fights that Ninth Tennessee troopers engaged in near Murfreesboro, Tennessee, in Decem-

ber 1863. Trooper John Weatherred was a participant: "We had many snow ball battles, four or five companies on each side. We had lively times for a day or two. The General [Braxton Bragg] stopped this snow ball war, but many of us had black and blue sore spots all over us."[121]

Money was at stake when soldiers gambled, a widespread activity that took many forms. Private John W. McCann of the Second Wisconsin explains that even officers gambled: "It is a common thing to see four officers sitting around an old greasy board with a deck of cards and three or four hundred dollars on the board. They keep the game agoing all day and all night. When one gets tired there is always more to take his place. All the officers do is gamble, drink whiskey and visit."[122]

And naturally, troopers loved to race their horses. A.E. Renfrow wrote from Fort Chadbourne, Texas, in 1862, "I have bin Horse racesing since I left home. I have Lost one hundred dollars an have got a race to be run on Saturday next I have got dick [his horse] bet on the race and if I loose him I will loose aheap more on the day of the race. I am going to win or loose something."[123] Racing became so distracting to the Texas Frontier Regiment that its commanding officer banned it.

Although many soldiers drank and gambled, others went to church.

A group of soldiers plays a friendly game of cards. Gambling was a common hobby for many troopers.

First New England bugler George Sargent's diary entry for May 8, 1864, offers an example of a military service: "Sunday. Had church services, as we do every sabbath when we are in camp. The services consist of a short sermon, generally containing some good advice by Parson Clark, a few psalm tunes by the band, and singing by the choir."[124]

LACK OF DISCIPLINE

Troopers sometimes left camp to have fun. Some departed even when they did not have permission, a practice called "running the guard" because they had to elude sentries. J.V. Hoakison remembers doing it when the Fourth Iowa was training in early 1862 near Mount Pleasant, Iowa: "I as well as many others in the Co. had many acquaintances in town among the young folks. So when it was dark I snuck out through the by-ways and alleys with the intention to go and see one of my best girls."[125] Hoakison had a good time but also the misfortune to be arrested on his return to camp.

Confederates left camp more often than Union troopers. Basil W. Duke, an officer who served under raider John Hunt Morgan, comments on the severity of the problem: "Camp guards were regularly posted to keep the men in camp, and as staying in camp closely was something they particularly disliked, the guard had to be doubled [several times], until finally nearly one half of the regiment had to be put on to watch the rest."[126]

The disregard for authority they showed by "running the guard" was just one indication of a glaring character defect Union and Confederate troopers shared—a lack of discipline. Although they followed orders in combat, at other times troopers often ignored regulations and treated their officers with contempt. This lack of discipline was common in all branches of the military. It was attributed to the fact that so many civilians

❧ CONFEDERATE LACK OF DISCIPLINE ❧

The lack of discipline by cavalrymen on both sides of the Civil War is legendary. In A Rebel's Recollections, *George Cary Eggleston of the First Virginia explains that for Confederate troopers part of their disdain for following orders was based on social standing. Like Eggleston, many Confederate troopers came from wealthy families that were considered the South's upper class; many of these men would not listen to an officer they believed to be socially inferior. Eggleston explains:*

The men who volunteered went to war of their own accord, and were wholly unaccustomed to acting on any other than their own [direction]. But they were not used to control of any sort, and were not disposed to obey anybody except for good and sufficient reason given. While actually on drill they obeyed the word of command, not so

much by reason of its being proper to obey a command, as because obedience was in that case necessary to the successful issue of a pretty performance in which they were interested. Off drill they did as they pleased, holding themselves gentlemen, and as such bound to consult only their own wills. There was one sort of rank, however, which was both maintained and respected from the first, namely, that of social life. The line of demarcation between gentry [upper-class citizens] and common people is not more sharply drawn anywhere than in Virginia. It rests there upon an indeterminate something or other, known as family. To come of a good family is a patent of nobility, and there is no other way whatever by which any man or any woman can find a passage into the charmed circle of Virginia's peerage.

had been rushed so quickly into the service that they had trouble adjusting to military life. "We had enlisted to put down the Rebellion," claimed Union trooper William R. Hartpence, "and had no patience with the red-tape tomfoolery of the regular service. Furthermore, our boys recognized no superiors, except in the line of legitimate duty [battle]."[127]

First Virginia's George Cary Eggleston believes part of the problem for Southern troopers was that many, like himself, were from wealthy families. These rich young men were accustomed to giving orders, not taking them, and to putting their own comfort ahead of someone else's, a state of mind that sometimes led them to treat officers rudely. Eggleston explains one incident: "I heard a gentleman without rank, who had brought a dispatch to [General] Stonewall Jackson, request that officer to 'cut the answer short,' on the ground that his horse was a little lame and he feared his inability to deliver it as promptly as was desirable."[128]

FURLOUGHS

A stay in camp was a treat for troopers, but being granted a furlough, formal permission to go home on leave, was like ascending to heaven. In February 1865 Samuel Cormany of the Sixteenth Pennsylvania was granted leave to visit his wife, Rachel, and young daughter, Cora, in Chambersburg, Pennsylvania. Cormany's diary for February 21 expresses his delight at seeing them again: "Pet [his wife] and Cora were there—well and happy and our meeting and greeting was never so sweet." Although the Cormanys enjoyed the reunion, Rachel complained in her diary for March 31 when Samuel went back: "I had a lonely ride coming home. Really it does not seem right that husbands should go and leave their wives. Such are the cruel fates of war."[129]

Many veterans on both sides were given furloughs as a bonus for reenlisting. James D. Sedinger and other members of the Eighth Virginia Cavalry, known as the Border Rangers, got a sixty-day leave when they signed up again in March 1864. Sedinger wrote that the rangers enjoyed their leave—"The boys all came home to the Border, and such a time the boys had"—but that when it ended, "there were many sad partings on that trip for the mothers all felt that it was the last time they would see their boys and with a good many it proved true—in fact too many."[130]

Many Confederates received furloughs so they could acquire new mounts. Although the Union provided cavalry horses, Southern troopers had to buy replacements if their horses died. This misguided policy resulted in so many leaves that many units did not have enough soldiers. In his diary for January 25, 1863, William Lyne Wilson of the Twelfth Virginia wrote that he paid $2,300 for a horse; before the war a good horse cost only about $100. But Wilson was glad to find a horse at any price, because troopers who could not find horses had to join the infantry. And as Wilson noted, "There is no predicament so disagreeable to a trooper—at least so far as my experience goes—as to be dismounted."[131]

MISSING LOVED ONES

Visits home were few and far too brief for soldiers who bitterly missed their loved ones. The only way to stay in touch with wives, parents, children, and friends was to write them, and troopers spent much of their spare time penning letters. George Kryder of the Third Ohio wrote over a hundred letters to his wife, Elizabeth. One letter dated March 14, 1862, from Tuscumbia, Alabama, describes the mental anguish soldiers experienced by being separated from family: "Felt very uneasy for about a week on account of a dream I had. I dreamed that I saw you in distress and weeping with your arms around my neck. Now I never believed much in dreams and I want you to let me know whether

Writing letters was the only way soldiers were able to keep in touch with loved ones.

you are in trouble about yourself or whether you are to be."[132]

Although their own lives were in danger, troopers often worried more about what would happen to loved ones. Twelfth Texas trooper Henry Orr explained to his father in an 1863 letter how thrilled he had been to receive mail from his brothers, James and Lafayette, who were in the infantry: "Oh! what a comfort to hear from my dear brothers [and know they still lived] who are battling in a far distant field."[133] And Absolom A. Harrison of the Fourth Kentucky wrote his wife, Martha, on January 19, 1862: "I would like to know how mother is and how you and the children are and if folks are getting along. I would like to be at home but I have got myself in this scrape and I will have to stand it."[134]

These mounted warriors, however, often bragged about their exploits. In a May 9, 1862, letter to his wife, Flora, four days after the Battle of Williamsburg, General James Ewell Brown (Jeb) Stuart boasted: "Blessed be the God that gives *us* the victory. The battle was a glorious affair. For myself I have only to say that if you had seen your husband you would have been proud of him. I was not out of fire the whole day."[135]

FRATERNIZING

Union and Confederate troopers, however, were not always shooting at each other. *Fraternizing* is a military term for friendly encounters with the enemy, and there were many such incidents in the Civil War. Most of these occurred when enemy soldiers were camped near each other but there was no major battle going on. Willard Glazier of the Second New York explains how Union and Confederate soldiers peacefully coexisted once while both sides were safely placed on separate sides of the Rappahannock River in Virginia. Writes Glazier:

The Federal and Rebel pickets mutually arranged that there shall be no firing on either side, unless an advance is undertaken. Squads of soldiers from both armies may be observed seated together on either side of the Rappahannock, earnestly discussing the great questions of the day. During all these interviews, trading was the order of the day, and a heavy business was carried in the tobacco, coffee, and hardtack line.[136]

The First Maine's Edward P. Tobie was part of that peaceful gathering. He remembers how the river failed to stop intraenemy commerce:

One method of sustaining commercial relations was to build a raft a foot or so square, generally of corn stalks, fix a mast

❧ CAVALRY VS. INFANTRY ❧

Although they fought on the same side, cavalry and infantry units in both the Union and Confederate armies did not get along with each other. In his twin books The Life of Billy Yank *and* The Life of Johnny Reb, *historian Bell Irvin Wiley discusses the jealousy and animosity that existed between the two branches of the military:*

[Union] infantrymen commonly regarded the cavalry as playboys who roamed the country at will, leaving to foot soldiers the mud, misery, and peril. Typical of the comments was made by Philip Smith while the army was en route from Mississippi to Chattanooga [Tennessee] in 1863: "We have considerable cavalry with us but they are the laughing stock of the army and the boys poke all kinds of fun at them. I really have as yet to see or hear of their doing anything of much credit to them."

Wiley explains that this interservice rivalry extended to the Confederates:

One of the aversions most frequent was of infantrymen for cavalrymen. The term "buttermilk cavalry" was universal among infantry. The connotation was apparently two-fold—foot soldiers thought the cavalry lazy because they rode and because they could beg or steal buttermilk and other delicacies. An Alabama soldier, James A. Hall, wrote April 18, 1864 [that] he thought every cavalry soldier should have a board tied to his back and the word "thief" written on it so good people might be on guard against them.

Wiley, however, notes that many infantry soldiers were simply jealous that they were not in the cavalry, which was considered easier duty and the elite branch of the military. He quotes a letter that Confederate infantryman Jerome Yates wrote to his mother in 1863 that includes some advice for his younger brother: "Tell Him to Join the Cavalry because being 'a private in The Infantry' *is the worse place he can possibly be put into in this war—so if he wants to have a good time Join the Cavalry."*

with a newspaper for a sail, load the raft with tobacco, and so set the sail that the wind would carry the raft across the river. The [Union] recipient would reciprocate in coffee and it was quite common, on asking a man where he got his tobacco, to receive the reply, "I had a ship come in."[137]

At times fraternization involved family members. DeWitt Clinton Gallaher, a courier with the First Virginia, remembers being asked to accompany Major Henry Brainerd

McClellan in early 1864 when he visited his brother, a Union captain, near Orange, Virginia. Although on opposite sides, the McClellans were from Philadelphia; the brothers wanted to meet because their sister had died. Gallaher rode to the meeting place with a white flag tied to his saber. Then, he wrote: "As the captain hurriedly dismounted the major rushed to him and soon they were locked in each other's arms and weeping. I shall never forget the pathetic sight of those two brothers sitting way off to themselves and sharing their sorrow at a sister's death and they situated as they were [as enemies]."[138]

SEEING ABE LINCOLN

One extra duty that troopers had in camp was having to parade before visiting dignitaries. First New England bugler George Sargent recounts the day President Abraham Lincoln reviewed almost twenty thousand soldiers. After helping play "Hail to the Chief," Sargent on April 6, 1863, had a chance to closely examine the president:

Abraham Lincoln pays a visit to Union troops. Entertaining visiting dignitaries was an extra duty soldiers had to perform in camp.

I must say he is the most awkward looking figure on horseback I ever saw, long legs, dangling down most to the ground, his body bent forward, looking as though he was about to pitch headlong, and an old stovepipe hat many years behind the fashion. We then formed in platoons and marched by him in review. As we got opposite him, we wheeled out and played until our brigade got by, then followed on behind. As we stood in front of him, I could not help but notice how pale, haggard, and careworn he looked, as though there was a heap of trouble on the old man's mind.[139]

The war had, indeed, taken its toll on Lincoln. But the conflict was just as hard on troopers on both sides who fought and lived under incredibly difficult conditions. Like Lincoln, they were only doing their duty.

MILITARY CAMPS

Military camps could house several hundred or even tens of thousands of soldiers. Many were temporary affairs, hastily assembled and just as quickly abandoned in line with the ebb and flow of battle. Most camps offered only the most basic amenities —shelter for soldiers, hospitals for medical care, and mess halls to serve meals. For the cavalry, there would also be blacksmiths to put new iron shoes on their horses and veterinarians to treat their mounts if they were ill.

In most camps, soldiers slept in tents. The most common model was the Sibley, which was patterned after cone-shaped Indian tepees and was large enough for a dozen troopers. Although tents were supposed to keep out rain and snow, Fifth Iowa captain Charles C. Nott admits they sometimes leaked:

> It is a rainy day in camp [Fort Henry in Tennessee]—since morning it has been rain, rain, rain. The camp seems deserted; save here and there you see a man, with blanket drawn close over head and shoulders, plod heavily and slowly through the mud. The horses stand with heads down, and drooping ears, stock still—nothing moves but the rain, and that straight down. The tents are tired of shedding rain, and it oozed through. There is water above, and mud beneath, and wet everywhere. No fun in soldiering now.[140]

During the coldest winter months, troopers built wooden roofs over tents and brought in stoves to stay warm and dry. In his diary for February 22, 1863, William Lyne Wilson of the Twelfth Virginia wrote: "This is the worst 22nd of February in my recollection. A cold driving snow all day

❧ WINTER QUARTERS ❧

During the coldest months of winter, most fighting ceased and soldiers moved into winter camps. When it was possible, they built permanent structures to house them against the cold so they would not have to rely only on their tents. In The Diary of a Bugler, *First New England bugler George Sargent describes the quarters that he and his comrades constructed:*

After working like beavers four or five days, got it completed. At home it would be called a good pigsty, but out here it is a palace. It is about 12 x 15 feet made of logs notched together, the cracks filled with mud. The roof is made of small poles laid close to-gether and covered with turf or sods. We have a fireplace in one corner and a chimney outside made of stones and mud topped with a barrel to make it draw well. Inside, we have two bunks made of poles covered with hay, one above the other, two occupying each. Over the fireplace is a mantelpiece on which may be found the ornaments peculiar to the cavalry service. Our door was made from a cracker box covered with a rubber [top] and hinges made from an old boot leg. The side of the door was a window sash, which one of the boys foraged from an empty house in the vicinity.

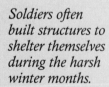
Soldiers often built structures to shelter themselves during the harsh winter months.

long, now covering the ground to the depth of 12 or 14 inches. Our old sibley is a 'friend in need' to us today and we hover closely around the camp stove, and bless its inventor."[141]

Even camps with wooden sleeping quarters were not always comfortable. Fourth Iowa trooper J.V. Hoakison remembers the unfriendly bedmates his regiment discovered the night of March 2, 1862, at Benton Barracks near St. Louis, Missouri:

We found that they were all occupied and running over with gray backs [lice]. For the first days and nights we were in terrible misery. It was a rub and scratch all the time until we became better acquainted with them. We remained here for two weeks and during this time we kept busy all the time in the daytime drilling and during the night fighting the gray backs and they got the best of [us] all the time.[142]

FILTHY CONDITIONS

Lice and other pesky insects were part of the squalor of military camps, which were generally filthy and inhabited by soldiers badly in need of a bath. After an inspection in January 1863 found many unwashed troopers, commanders of the First Massachusetts warned the regiment's officers they would be "held to a strict responsibility for the cleanliness of their men. Today is warm enough for an improvement in this respect [by having the men wash]. The necks, faces, and hands of the men are very dirty."[143]

Union officers ordered soldiers to bathe and air their bedding weekly, something many did not do in an era

Washing clothes and keeping clean was very important for soldiers, since lack of hygiene invited lice and other insects.

when cleanliness was not highly prized. However, it was often difficult for soldiers to stay clean. In a letter Henry Orr of the Twelfth Texas wrote to his mother on January 22, 1862, he complained: "It seems impossible for us to get soap enough; we only get a little occasionally, consequently we can't keep clean."[144]

An additional sanitation problem for cavalry was their horse barns, which troopers sometimes neglected. When the First New York was criticized for its filthy stables in July 1862, Commander W.W. Averell responded that the animal waste and other debris would be cleaned up: "I regret exceeding that there should have been any grounds for complaints of the condition of the police [sanitation], &c., of the 1st New York. I have now a hundred [men working with] spades at work, and will soon present the brigade in an improved condition."[145] Eighth Illinois surgeon Abner Hard noted that First New York troopers camped near his hospital had "left their dead horses lay in close proximity to us, until we were obliged to complain to their colonel to abate the nuisance."[146]

Some Confederate troopers from wealthy families had an easier time with such chores; their servants did the work. George Cary Eggleston of the First Virginia explains: "Whenever a detail was made for the purpose of cleaning the campground, the men detailed regarded themselves as responsible for the proper performance of the task by their servants [slaves], and uncomplainingly took upon themselves the duty of sitting on the fence and superintending the work."[147]

MEDICAL CARE

Poor sanitation and hygiene made many camps unhealthy places, with filth and contaminated water and food causing illnesses like typhoid fever. The close proximity of thousands of men also allowed measles, smallpox, and other contagious diseases to quickly spread. Archibald Atkinson Jr., a surgeon with the Virginia cavalry, remembers one such wave of illness: "There was an epidemic of measles in the army & every soldier who had not been 10 miles from his home before he enlisted [and thus had not been exposed to measles] was seized with it. I've had boys of 16, & fathers of 60 years lying side by side on straw beds placed on the floor all suffering from measles."[148]

The medical problems were most severe the first year of the war before troopers learned how to keep their new military homes clean. Hard noted that in January 1862 more than five hundred soldiers in his regiment were sick, most with typhoid fever. "We had but two hospital tents," he writes, "and consequently were

⚜ SICK CALL WITH THE TEXAS CAVALRY ⚜

Cavalry doctors who cared for troopers often did not have the knowledge or proper medicine to adequately treat them. In The Lone Star Defenders: A Chronicle of the Third Texas Cavalry Regiment in the Civil War, *Samuel B. Barron of the Third Texas explains how Dr. Wallace McDugald diagnosed and treated soldiers during daily sick call, when soldiers lined up to explain what ailed them:*

He would walk out with an old jack-knife in his hand, and conveniently located just behind him could be seen a lump of opium as big as a cannonball. Beginning at the head of the line he would say to the first one: "Well, sir, what is the matter with *you?*" "I don't know, doctor; I've got a pain in my back, a hurting in my stomach, or a misery in my head, or I had a chill last night." "Let me see your tongue. How's your bowels?" He would then turn around and vigorously attack the lump of opium with his knife, and roll out from two to four pills to the man, remarking to each of his waiting patients: "Here, take one of these every two hours." Thus he would go, down the line to the end, and in all there was little variation—none to speak of except in the answers of the individuals, the number of pills, or the manner of taking. And what else could he do? He had told me he had no medicine except opium.

obliged to send a large number to the general hospital in Alexandria [Virginia], where many of them died."[149]

Hard must have hated sending men there because the overcrowded, understaffed army hospitals were not very good. When Fifth Iowa captain Charles C. Nott visited some of his men who had measles, he was appalled at conditions in the hospital:

As I looked around, I learned why soldiers dread the hospital. The cots were close together, with just room enough to pass between, and on every cot lay a sick man. At the sound of the opening door, some looked eagerly toward us—others turned their eyes languidly—and others again did not change their vacant gaze, too weak to care who came or went away. There were faces flushed with fever, others pale and thin, and others with the pallor of death settling upon them.[150]

Civil War medical care was primitive. Many army doctors were poorly trained, and even in camp they had few reliable medicines to treat their patients; the most common medication was opium, a drug freely distributed to ease pain, fever, and other symptoms for a wide variety of illnesses. Atkinson explains that it was even harder caring for troopers in the field: "There was a man always detailed to accompany me to carry the knapsack containing bandages, pocket case of instruments, & a small amputating case. In cavalry we could do less for our wounded than in infantry, for the cavalry troops are the eyes & ears for the army, & we [are] usually on the move."[151]

Disease and other causes, often poor medical treatment, killed more than twice as many men as combat did. Of the estimated 620,000 Americans who died in the Civil War, battle deaths accounted for 204,070 deaths —110,070 Union, 94,000 Confederate —while 250,152 Northern and 164,000 Southern soldiers died of disease and other causes, such as accidents like being run over by a wagon.

As Atkinson noted, it was often harder for troopers than for sick or wounded infantrymen to receive medical care because their duties kept them away from camp so much. Troopers also did not enjoy the luxury of lounging around camp between battles or always having food provided for them. But such was the life these mounted warriors had chosen, and they had no choice but to accept the hardships that accompanied their role in fighting the Civil War.

CONCLUSION

THE CAVALRY RIDES HOME

The Civil War came to a close on April 9, 1865, when General Robert E. Lee, a West Point graduate and former Union cavalry officer, surrendered to General Ulysses S. Grant at Appomattox Courthouse in Virginia. When Samuel B. Barron of the Third Texas Cavalry learned the fighting had ended, he was relieved: "The four years of war, with all its fun and frolic, all its hardships and privations, its advances and retreats, its victories and defeats, its killing and maiming was at an end."[152] Barron returned to Cherokee County in Texas to study law and eventually was elected county judge.

For Barron and other troopers, their cavalry days were something they would cherish in their minds and hearts all the days of their lives. But far too many soldiers did not return. When William Thomas of the Ninth Pennsylvania arrived home

August 1, 1865, he noted in his diary, "My Friends Were Glad to see me Come, but There were some Sad Faces for Them that did not Come [back]."[153] The combined 618,222 Civil War fatalities—360,222 Union soldiers and 258,000 Confederates—is greater than the total number of soldiers who died in every other U.S. war from the American Revolution through the Korean War.

But even for those lucky enough to make it back, postwar life was not always easy. Especially for those on the losing side.

CONFEDERATE TROOPERS

Confederates returned to areas devastated by war, many to discover their own homes destroyed. But thanks to Lee, a former trooper himself, they still had their horses. In negotiating surrender terms, Lee persuaded Grant not to confiscate all Confederate horses: "General, our cavalrymen furnish their own horses, they are not Government horses. Some of them may be, but of course you will find them out—any property that is [Confederate] property, you will ascertain that, but it is nearly all private property, and these men will want to plough ground and plant corn."[154]

Grant approved the request, and for many Southern troopers their horse was almost all they had left. William L. Royall of the Ninth Virginia returned home to find that Mount Ephraim, his family's Virginia plantation, had been robbed of its livestock and wealth by Union soldiers. "I went to work as a common laborer on the farm [family land] and labored there two years, by which time I had pulled the place up so that my mother and her family could get a very good living out of it,"[155] said Royall. Three years later he went to Richmond and became a lawyer.

The war left many Confederates bitter. One of them was General Nathan Bedford Forrest, who after returning to his ruined cotton plantation in Sunflower Landing, Mississippi, wrote, "I came out of the war pretty well wrecked, completely used up, shot all to pieces, crippled up . . . a beggar."[156] Forrest became wealthy again building railroads, but he was also angry about how the United

Nathan Bedford Forrest leads Confederate cavalrymen in an attack on unarmed black Union soldiers. Forrest later became the first Grand Wizard of the Ku Klux Klan.

States was governing the South. In 1867 he helped organize the Ku Klux Klan and was its first Grand Wizard, or leader. At first the Klan opposed U.S. policies it believed to be unfair to Southerners, but it degenerated into a racist group dedicated to oppressing African Americans and denying them their rights.

Southern troopers who felt they had failed to protect their homeland often worried about how future generations would remember them. A.W. Sparks of the Ninth Texas wrote that he hoped descendants of Confederate soldiers would realize they were "children of patriots [who fought] for liberty and for right and who are proud of their record."[157]

UNION TROOPERS

For thousands of Union troopers, however, the fighting was not over. At the end of the Civil War, the United States needed cavalry in the West, where Indian unrest against an increasing flood of settlers had escalated. The U.S. government forced soldiers whose war enlistments had not ended to man frontier outposts.

This enraged many soldiers, and hundreds of them deserted. When the Sixth Michigan was sent to Fort Leavenworth, Kansas, Brigadier General James Kidd tried to calm troopers by explaining that their country still needed them. In his diary trooper Franklin P. Grommon

relates Kidd's message: "He says we will have to stay our time out now & he said that it was orders from the war Department that we should, it don't look right but we must stand it seems for [a] few months longer, then we hope they will be content to let us go home in piece [*sic*]."[158]

For officers like George Armstrong Custer, however, the army was their career. In July 1866 Custer became a lieutenant colonel in the new Seventh Cavalry. It was while leading 250 troopers of the Seventh Cavalry that he was killed on June 25, 1876, in the Battle of the Little Bighorn, the most famous single battle ever fought between the cavalry and Indians.

Union troopers who did go home returned with the satisfaction of having served their country. Cornelius Baker of the Ninth Pennsylvania lived nearly six decades after the fighting stopped. He married three times, had several children (one of whom, Edward, died while fighting in the Spanish-American War in 1898 in the Philippines), and was a building contractor. Like all soldiers, he never forgot the war. The last words Baker uttered before he died on September 2, 1923, were "I have done my duty as an American citizen."[159]

THE DEATH OF ROMANCE

The surrender at Appomattox ended not only the Civil War but the most

Many soldiers who first envisioned themselves as chivalrous knights (left) soon were disillusioned by the grim, violent reality of the Civil War (right).

important period in U.S. Cavalry history. Historian Gregory J. Urwin claims that the conflict "marked the highest position the pony soldier [troopers] would ever hold in American military practice. More Americans fought from horseback during this war than in any struggle before or since."[160]

Urwin also argues that the war changed the basic role the cavalry played in combat—troopers had shown they were more valuable as mobile dismounted fighters than mounted warriors—as well as the way the public viewed this branch of the military. Urwin writes that the romantic notions Americans once held about cavalry service had died as surely as had tens of thousands of troopers in the war's grim fighting:

The War Between the States marked both the apotheosis and demise of the cavalier tradition that was so dear to Americans of the first half of the nineteenth century. In those early days [of the war], thousands of youngsters rode from their sheltered homes in plumed hats and tight, elegant uniforms, envisioning themselves as chivalrous knights errant, setting forth on the high road of honor to give battle with gleaming blades. By the end of the contest, those who survived had been converted to drab mounted infantry, who did their killing with revolvers and repeating carbines.[161]

INTRODUCTION: THE ROMANCE OF THE CAVALRY

1. Quoted in John W. Rowell, *Yankee Cavalrymen: Through the Civil War with the Ninth Pennsylvania Cavalry.* Knoxville: University of Tennessee Press, 1971, p. 14.
2. Quoted in John Q. Anderson, ed., *Campaigning with Parsons' Texas Cavalry Brigade, C.S.A.: The War Journal and Letters of the Four Orr Brothers, 12th Texas Cavalry Regiment.* Waco, TX: Hill Junior College Press, 1967, p. 1.
3. Quoted in New Hampshire Volunteer Cavalry. www.members.comptek.net.
4. Edward P. Tobie, *History of the First Maine Cavalry.* Boston: First Maine Cavalry Association, 1887, pp. 3–4.
5. Quoted in John W. Thomason Jr., *Jeb Stuart.* New York: Charles Scribner's Sons, 1929, p. 294.
6. Quoted in Fairfax Downey, *Clash of Cavalry: The Battle of Brandy Station, June 9, 1863.* New York: David McKay, 1959, p. 212.
7. Quoted in Edward G. Longacre, *Lincoln's Cavalrymen: A History of the Mounted Forces of the Army of the Potomac, 1861–1865.* Mechanicsburg, PA: Stackpole Books, 2000, p. 29.
8. Quoted in Anderson, *Campaigning with Parsons' Texas Cavalry Brigade,* p. 62.
9. Quoted in Orr Kelly and Mary Davies Kelly, *Dream's End: Two Iowa Brothers in the Civil War.* New York: Kodansha America, 1998, p. 197.
10. Quoted in Andrew Carroll, ed., *War Letters: Extraordinary Correspondence from American Wars.* New York: Scribner, 2001, p. 70.

CHAPTER 1: RECRUITING AND TRAINING THE CAVALRY

11. Quoted in Longacre, *Lincoln's Cavalrymen,* p. 31.
12. Quoted in Stephen Z. Starr, *The Union Cavalry in the Civil War, Vol. 1: From Fort Sumter to Gettysburg.* Baton Rouge: Louisiana State University Press, 1979, p. 212.
13. J.H. Kidd, *Personal Recollections of a Cavalryman: With Custer's Michigan Cavalry Brigade in the Civil War.* Grand Rapids, MI: Black Letter Press, 1969, p. 40.

14. Quoted in "Cavalry Tactics in the American Civil War." www.users.aol.com.

15. Quoted in Gregory J. Urwin, *The United States Cavalry: An Illustrated History.* New York: Sterling, 1983, p. 117.

16. Quoted in Festus P. Summers, ed., *A Borderland Confederate.* Pittsburgh: University of Pittsburgh Press, 1962, p. 127.

17. Quoted in *The History or Biography of J.V. Hoakison During the War of the Rebellion.* www.iowa3rdcavalry.com.

18. Quoted in Starr, *The Union Cavalry in the Civil War,* p. 110.

19. Tobie, *History of the First Maine Cavalry,* p. 24.

20. Quoted in Rowell, *Yankee Cavalrymen,* p. 14.

21. Quoted in Rowell, *Yankee Cavalrymen,* p. 25.

22. Quoted in Theophilus F. Rodenbough, ed., *The Photographic History of the Civil War, Vol. 2: The Cavalry.* New York: Fairfax Press, 1983, p. 60.

23. Quoted in Starr, *The Union Cavalry in the Civil War,* p. 136.

24. Quoted in Longacre, *Lincoln's Cavalrymen,* p. 35.

25. Quoted in Starr, *The Union Cavalry in the Civil War,* p. 133.

26. Quoted in James M. Merrill, *Spurs to Glory: The Story of the United States Cavalry.* Chicago: Rand McNally, 1966, p. 124.

27. Quoted in Starr, *The Union Cavalry in the Civil War,* p. 110.

28. Willard Glazier, *Three Years in the Federal Cavalry.* New York: Harper & Brothers, 1866, p. 35.

29. Quoted in The First Maine Cavalry. www.state.me.us.

30. George Cary Eggleston, *A Rebel's Recollections.* docsouth.unc.edu.

31. Eggleston, *A Rebel's Recollections*

32. Quoted in Downey, *Clash of Cavalry,* p. 18.

33. Quoted in Samuel Carter III, *The Last Cavaliers: Confederate and Union Cavalry in the Civil War.* New York: St. Martin's Press, 1979, p. 7.

34. Quoted in Patrick Brennan, "The Best Cavalry in the World," *North & South,* January 1999, p. 13.

35. Quoted in Anderson, *Campaigning with Parsons' Texas Cavalry Brigade,* p. 12.

36. William Lawrence Royall, *Some Reminiscences.* docsouth.unc.edu.

37. Quoted in Rowell, *Yankee Cavalrymen,* p. 33.

38. Quoted in the 8th NY—Newspaper Report. www.geocities.com.

39. Quoted in Anderson, *Campaigning with Parsons' Texas Cavalry Brigade,* p. 4.

Chapter 2: Life in the Saddle: The Varied Duties of the Cavalry Trooper

40. Quoted in Rodenbough, *The Photographic History of the Civil War,* p. 62.

41. Quoted in Anderson, *Campaigning with Parsons' Texas Cavalry Brigade,* p. 65.

42. Quoted in Rowell, *Yankee Cavalrymen,* p. 40.

43. Quoted in Bell Irvin Wiley, *The Life of Johnny Reb: The Common Soldier of the Confederacy.* Baton Rouge: Louisiana State University Press, 1978, p. 24.

44. Tobie, *History of the First Maine Cavalry,* p. 125.

45. Rodenbough, *The Photographic History of the Civil War,* p. 85.

46. Quoted in Lee Jacobs, ed., *Cry Heart.* Camden, SC: John Culler & Sons, 1995, p. 73.

47. Quoted in Carroll, *War Letters,* p. 65.

48. Glazier, *Three Years in the Federal Cavalry,* pp. 54–55.

49. Glazier, *Three Years in the Federal Cavalry,* p. 140.

50. Quoted in Starr, *The Union Cavalry in the Civil War,* p. 250.

51. Quoted in Rodenbough, *The Photographic History of the Civil War,* p. 214.

52. Charles C. Nott, *Sketches of War: Letters to the North Moore Street School of New York.* New York: Anson D.F. Randolph, 1865, p. 27.

53. Tobie, *History of the First Maine Cavalry,* p. 125.

54. Quoted in Martha L. Crabb, *All Afire to Fight: The Untold Tale of the Civil War's Ninth Texas Cavalry.* New York: Avon Books, 2000, p. 165.

55. Abner Hard, *History of the Eighth Cavalry Regiment, Illinois Volunteers.* Aurora, IL.: n.p., 1868, p. 222.

56. Quoted in Wiley, *The Life of Johnny Reb,* p. 46.

57. Quoted in Downey, *Clash of Cavalry,* p. 32.

58. Quoted in Downey, *Clash of Cavalry,* p. 28.

59. Quoted in Starr, *The Union Cavalry in the Civil War,* p. 110.

60. Rodenbough, *The Photographic History of the Civil War,* p. 32.

61. Starr, "Cavalry Tactics in the American Civil War."

62. Royall, *Some Reminiscences.*

63. Nott, *Sketches of War,* p. 43.

64. Quoted in "General John Buford's Cavalry in the Gettysburg Campaign." www.bufordsboys.com.

CHAPTER 3: CAVALRY RAIDERS AND GUERRILLAS

65. Rodenbough, *The Photographic History of the Civil War,* p. 116.

66. John W. Munson, *Reminiscences of a Mosby Raider.* Washington, DC: Zenger Publishing, 1982, p. 221.

67. Quoted in Carter, *The Last Cavaliers,* p. 16.

68. Quoted in Robert J. Trout, *They Followed the Plume: J.E.B. Stuart and His Staff.* Mechanicsburg, PA: Stackpole Books, 1993, p. 2.

69. Rodenbough, *The Photographic History of the Civil War,* p. 85.

70. Quoted in John K. Herr and Edward S. Wallace, *The Story of the U.S. Cavalry.* Boston: Little, Brown, 1953, p. 100.

71. Quoted in Rod Gragg, ed., *The Illustrated Confederate Reader.* New York: Harper & Row, 1989, p. 199.

72. Quoted in Jeffry D. Wert, *Mosby's*

Rangers. New York: Simon and Schuster, 1990, p. 34.

73. Quoted in Wert, *Mosby's Rangers,* p. 22.

74. Munson, *Reminiscences of a Mosby Raider,* pp. 12, 21.

75. Quoted in Rowell, *Yankee Cavalrymen,* p. 95.

76. Quoted in Starr, *The Union Cavalry in the Civil War,* p. 356.

77. Tobie, *History of the First Maine Cavalry,* p. 143.

78. Quoted in Carter, *The Last Cavaliers,* p. 131.

79. Starr, "Cavalry Tactics in the American Civil War."

80. Memoir of Archibald Atkinson Jr. www.scholar2.lib.vt.edu.

81. Quoted in Longacre, *Lincoln's Cavalrymen,* p. 272.

82. Longacre, *Lincoln's Cavalrymen,* p. 272.

83. Quoted in Rowell, *Yankee Cavalrymen,* p. 39.

84. Quoted in Starr, *The Union Cavalry in the Civil War,* p. 258.

85. Quoted in Jacobs, *Cry Heart,* p. 270.

86. Quoted in Samuel J. Martin, "What Was Judson Kilpatrick's Secret?" *Civil War Times,* February 2000, p. 23.

87. "Bushwhackers & Jayhawkers: Uncivil Missouri & Kansas." www. umkc.edu.

88. Quoted in Thomas Goodrich, *Black Flag: Guerrilla Warfare on the Western Border, 1861–1865.* Bloomington: Indiana University Press, 1995, p. 39.

89. Quoted in Goodrich, *Black Flag,* p. 16.

90. Quoted in Jacobs, *Cry Heart,* p. 277.

CHAPTER 4: CAVALRY SOLDIERS IN COMBAT

91. Quoted in Merrill, *Spurs to Glory,* p. 150.

92. Quoted in Carter, *The Last Cavaliers,* p. 159.

93. Merrill, *Spurs to Glory,* p. 123.

94. Urwin, *The United States Cavalry,* p. 133.

95. Quoted in Starr, *The Union Cavalry in the Civil War,* p. 124.

96. Quoted in Bell Irvin Wiley, *The Life of Billy Yank: The Common Soldier of the Union.* Baton Rouge: Louisiana State University Press, 1971, p. 64.

97. Quoted in Urwin, *The United States Cavalry,* p. 114.

98. Samuel B. Barron, *The Lone Star Defenders: A Chronicle of the Third Texas Cavalry Regiment in the Civil War.* Washington, DC: Zenger Publishing, 1983, p. 28.

99. Munson, *Reminiscences of a Mosby Raider,* p. 23.

100. Quoted in Robert W. Wells, *Wisconsin in the Civil War.* Milwaukee: Journal Company, 1964, p. 42.

101. Royall, *Some Reminiscences.*

102. Quoted in Trout, *They Followed the Plume,* p. 135.

103. Quoted in Urwin, *The United States Cavalry,* p. 108.

104. Quoted in Starr, *The Union Cavalry in the Civil War,* p. 65.

105. Quoted in Rodenbough, *The Photographic History of the Civil War,* p. 248.

106. Quoted in Lawrence D. Schiller, "A Taste of Northern Steel: The Evolution of Federal Cavalry Tactics 1861–1865," *North & South,* January 1999, p. 42.

107. Quoted in Edward G. Longacre, *Custer and His Wolverines: The Michigan Cavalry Brigade 1861–1865.* Conshohocken, PA: Combined Publishing, 1997, p. 9.

108. Quoted in Thomason, *Jeb Stuart,* p. 228.

109. "An account written by Major H. B. McClellan after General Stuart's death at Yellow Tavern." www.sw civilwar.com.

110. *Wartime Diary of John Weatherred* www.jackmasters.net.

111. Quoted in Rowell, *Yankee Cavalrymen,* p. 55.

112. Quoted in Carter, *The Last Cavaliers,* p. 175.

113. Quoted in Howard Coffin, *Full Duty: Vermonters in the Civil War.* Woodstock, VT: Countryman Press, 1993, p. 199.

114. Quoted in Rodenbough, *The Photographic History of the Civil War,* p. 240.

115. Quoted in Downey, *Clash of Cavalry,* p. 147.

116. George Sargent, *The Diary of a Bugler.* members.comptek.net.

CHAPTER 5: NONCOMBAT LIFE OF THE CAVALRY

117. *The Diary of a Bugler* by George Sargent.

118. Quoted in Anderson, *Campaigning with Parsons' Texas Cavalry Brigade,* p. 65.

119. Randolph Harrison McKim, *A Soldier's Recollections: Leaves from the Diary of a Young Confederate, with an Oration on the Motives and Aims of the Soldiers of the South.* docsouth.unc.edu.

120. Quoted in Anderson, *Campaigning with Parsons' Texas Cavalry Brigade,* p. 65.

121. *Wartime Diary of John Weatherred.*

122. Quoted in Wells, *Wisconsin in the Civil War,* p. 30.

123. Quoted in Wiley, *The Life of Johnny Reb,* p. 38.

124. *The Diary of a Bugler* by George Sargent.

125. The History or Biography of J.V. Hoakison During the War of the Rebellion.

126. Quoted in "Cavalry Tactics in the American Civil War."

127. Quoted in Starr, *The Union Cavalry in the Civil War,* pp. 166–67.

128. Eggleston, *A Rebel's Recollections.*

129. Quoted in James C. Mohr, ed., *The Cormany Diaries: A Northern Family in the Civil War.* Pittsburgh: University of Pittsburgh Press, 1982, pp. 521, 529.

130. "War-Time Reminiscences of James

D. Sedinger, Company E, 8th Virginia Cavalry (Border Rangers)." www.wvculture.org.

131. Quoted in Summers, *A Borderland Confederate*, p. 43.

132. George Kryder Papers. www.bgsu.edu.

133. Quoted in Anderson, *Campaigning with Parsons' Texas Cavalry Brigade*, p. 118.

134. Absolom A. Harrison Letters. www.civilwarhome.com.

135. Quoted in Thomason, *Jeb Stuart*, p. 136.

136. Glazier, *Three Years in the Federal Cavalry*, p. 18.

137. Tobie, *History of the First Maine Cavalry*, p. 110.

138. Quoted in Trout, *They Followed the Plume*, p. 199.

139. *The Diary of a Bugler* by George Sargent.

140. Nott, *Sketches of War*, p. 56.

141. Quoted in Summers, *A Borderland Confederate*, p. 48.

142. The History or Biography of J.V. Hoakison During the War of the Rebellion.

143. Quoted in Starr, *The Union Cavalry in the Civil War*, p. 175.

144. Quoted in Anderson, *Campaigning with Parsons' Texas Cavalry Brigade*, p. 23.

145. Quoted in Starr, *The Union Cavalry in the Civil War*, p. 267.

146. Hard, *History of the Eighth Cavalry Regiment*, p. 138.

147. Eggleston, *A Rebel's Recollections*.

148. Memoir of Archibald Atkinson, Jr.

149. Hard, *History of the Eighth Cavalry Regiment*, p. 169.

150. Nott, *Sketches of War*, p. 12.

151. Memoir of Archibald Atkinson, Jr.

CONCLUSION: THE CAVALRY RIDES HOME

152. Quoted in Crabb, *All Afire to Fight*, p. 297.

153. Quoted in Rowell, *Yankee Cavalrymen*, p. 255.

154. Quoted in Henry Steele Commager, *The Blue and the Gray; The Story of the Civil War as Told by Its Participants*. New York: Fairfax Press, 1982, p. 1,140.

155. Royall, *Some Reminiscences*.

156. Quoted in Carter, *The Last Cavaliers*, p. 318.

157. Quoted in Crabb, *All Afire to Fight*, p. 304.

158. Quoted in Longacre, *Custer and His Wolverines*, p. 284.

159. Quoted in Rowell, *Yankee Cavalrymen*, p. 264.

160. Urwin, *The United States Cavalry*, p. 108.

161. Urwin, *The United States Cavalry*, p. 108.

FOR FURTHER READING

John Q. Anderson, ed., *Campaigning with Parsons' Texas Cavalry Brigade, C.S.A.: The War Journal and Letters of the Four Orr Brothers, 12th Texas Cavalry Regiment.* Waco, TX: Hill Junior College Press, 1967. First-person accounts provide a personal and interesting view of cavalry life.

Samuel Carter III, *The Last Cavaliers: Confederate and Union Cavalry in the Civil War.* New York: St. Martin's Press, 1979. The author paints a vivid picture of the personalities of many of the top cavalry leaders.

Fairfax Downey, *Clash of Cavalry: The Battle of Brandy Station, June 9, 1863.* New York: David McKay, 1959. The author reviews not only the war's most famous cavalry battle but the history of mounted warfare in America.

Edward G. Longacre, *Lincoln's Cavalrymen: A History of the Mounted Forces of the Army of the Potomac, 1861–1865.* Mechanicsburg, PA: Stackpole Books, 2000. A well-documented history by one of the most knowledgeable experts on the U.S. Cavalry.

James C. Mohr, ed., *The Cormany Diaries: A Northern Family in the Civil War.* Pittsburgh: University of Pittsburgh Press, 1982. Diaries kept by Sixteenth Pennsylvania trooper Samuel Cormany and his wife, Rachel, during the Civil War.

Theophilus F. Rodenbough, ed., *The Photographic History of the Civil War, Vol. 2: The Cavalry.* New York: Fairfax Press, 1983. Published originally in 1911, its pictures provide an unsurpassed view of cavalry life.

WORKS CONSULTED

BOOKS

Samuel B. Barron, *The Lone Star Defenders: A Chronicle of the Third Texas Cavalry Regiment in the Civil War.* Washington, DC: Zenger Publishing, 1983. First published in 1908, this regimental history is colorful and informative.

Andrew Carroll, ed., *War Letters: Extraordinary Correspondence from American Wars.* New York: Scribner, 2001. Letters from soldiers from various wars provide interesting insights into their lives.

Howard Coffin, *Full Duty: Vermonters in the Civil War.* Woodstock, VT: Countryman Press, 1993. The author details the part Vermont soldiers played in the war.

Henry Steele Commager, *The Blue and the Gray; The Story of the Civil War as Told by Its Participants.* New York: Fairfax Press, 1982. This book uses primary sources to tell the story of individual soldiers in the war.

Philip St. George Cooke, *Cavalry Tactics: Regulations for the Instruction, Formations & Movements, the Cavalry of the Army and Volunteers of the United States.* New York: J.W. Fortune, 1862. The standard cavalry manual during the war.

Martha L. Crabb, *All Afire to Fight: The Untold Tale of the Civil War's Ninth Texas Cavalry.* New York: Avon Books, 2000. The author explains what the regiment did and how troopers reacted to war.

Willard Glazier, *Three Years in the Federal Cavalry.* New York: Harper & Brothers, 1866. An interesting look at cavalry life and the Civil War.

Thomas Goodrich, *Black Flag: Guerrilla Warfare on the Western Border, 1861–1865.* Bloomington: Indiana University Press, 1995. A vivid portrait of guerrilla warfare during the Civil War.

Rod Gragg, ed., *The Illustrated Confederate Reader.* New York: Harper & Row, 1989. Diaries, letters, and other primary sources tell the stories of Confederate soldiers in the war.

Abner Hard, *History of the Eighth Cavalry Regiment, Illinois Volunteers.* Aurora, IL.: n.p., 1868. This history by the regiment's surgeon contains vivid descriptions of Civil War medical care.

John K. Herr and Edward S. Wallace, *The Story of the U.S. Cavalry.* Boston: Little, Brown, 1953. A solid history of the U.S. Cavalry.

Lee Jacobs, ed., *Cry Heart.* Camden, SC: John Culler & Sons, 1995. Personal accounts of the experiences of Confederate soldiers and civilians.

Orr Kelly and Mary Davies Kelly, *Dream's End: Two Iowa Brothers in the Civil War.* New York: Kodansha America, 1998. Contains some interesting personal accounts of cavalry life.

J. H. Kidd, *Personal Recollections of a Cavalryman: With Custer's Michigan Cavalry Brigade in the Civil War.* Grand Rapids, MI: Black Letter Press, 1969. First printed in 1908, Kidd provides interesting commentary on cavalry life.

Edward G. Longacre, *Custer and His Wolverines: The Michigan Cavalry Brigade 1861–1865.* Conshohocken, PA: Combined Publishing, 1997. An informative history of Custer's actions in the war.

James M. Merrill, *Spurs to Glory: The Story of the United States Cavalry.* Chicago: Rand McNally, 1966. An interesting account of U.S. Cavalry history.

John W. Munson, *Reminiscences of a Mosby Raider.* Washington, DC: Zenger Publishing, 1982. First published in 1906, a vivid description of what it was like to ride with Mosby.

Charles C. Nott, *Sketches of War: Letters to the North Moore Street School of New York.* New York: Anson D.F. Randolph, 1865. Letters a Union officer wrote to students from the battlefield provide an unusual view of cavalry life.

John W. Rowell, *Yankee Cavalrymen: Through the Civil War with the Ninth Pennsylvania Cavalry.* Knoxville: University of Tennessee Press, 1971. An intimate look at the lives of Pennsylvania troopers.

William Forse Scott, *The Story of a Cavalry Regiment.* New York: G.P. Putnam's Sons, 1893. This regimental history offers a good look at how troopers did their job.

Stephen Z. Starr, *The Union Cavalry in the Civil War, Vol. 1: From Fort Sumter to Gettysburg.* Baton Rouge: Louisiana State University Press, 1979. His three-volume history is the definitive study of the U.S. Cavalry in the Civil War.

Festus P. Summers, ed., *A Borderland Confederate.* Pittsburgh: University of Pittsburgh Press, 1962. The diaries and letters of William L. Wilson tell the exciting story of his days as a trooper.

John W. Thomason Jr., *Jeb Stuart.* New York: Charles Scribner's Sons, 1929. One of the finest biographies of this Confederate hero.

Edward P. Tobie, *History of the First Maine Cavalry.* Boston: First Maine Cavalry Association, 1887. An interesting regimental history written by a colorful writer.

Robert J. Trout, *They Followed the Plume: J.E.B. Stuart and His Staff.* Mechanicsburg, PA: Stackpole Books, 1993. The author uses many primary sources from Stuart's staff members to tell their stories.

Gregory J. Urwin, *The United States Cavalry: An Illustrated History.* New York: Sterling, 1983. A well-documented study of the U.S. Cavalry throughout its history.

Robert W. Wells, *Wisconsin in the Civil War.* Milwaukee: Journal Company, 1964. This compilation of *Milwaukee Journal* newspaper articles has many interesting facts and stories about the war.

Jeffry D. Wert, *Mosby's Rangers.* New York: Simon and Schuster, 1990. A well-documented account of the actions of Mosby and his men.

Bell Irvin Wiley, *The Life of Billy Yank: The Common Soldier of the Union.* Baton Rouge: Louisiana State University Press, 1971. An interesting, well-documented study of what daily life was like for Union soldiers in the Civil War.

————, *The Life of Johnny Reb: The Common Soldier of the Confederacy.* Baton Rouge: Louisiana State University Press, 1978. An interesting, well-documented study of what daily life was like for Confederate soldiers in the Civil War.

PERIODICALS

Patrick Brennan, "The Best Cavalry in the World," *North & South,* January 1999.

Leona M. Dillard, "Massacre without Tomahawks," *Midwest Quarterly,* Spring 1997.

Samuel J. Martin, "What Was Judson Kilpatrick's Secret?" *Civil War Times,* February 2000.

Lawrence D. Schiller, "A Taste of Northern Steel: The Evolution of Federal Cavalry Tactics 1861–1865," *North & South,* January 1999.

INTERNET SOURCES

"About the Cavalry Horse by Cap. Charles Francis Adams." www.geo cities.com. An Internet site by the Seventeenth Pennsylvania Cavalry, a reenacted group.

Absolom A. Harrison Letters. www. civilwarhome.com. A Civil War Internet site.

An account written by Major H.B. McClellan after General Stuart's death at Yellow Tavern. www.swcivilwar. com. Civil War Internet site.

"Bushwhackers & Jayhawkers: Uncivil Missouri & Kansas." www.umkc.edu. An Internet site of the University of Missouri–Kansas City's School of Education.

"Cavalry Tactics in the American Civil War." www.users.aol.com. An explanation of tactics by Civil War historian Stephen Z. Starr, based on a report to the Cincinnati Civil War Round Table.

The Diary of a Bugler by George Sargent. members.comptek.net. An Internet site devoted to the Civil War.

"8th NY—Newspaper Report." www.geo cities.com. A collection of letters that the Eighth New York Cavalry sent home to the *Rochester Daily Union and Advertiser newspaper.*

The First Maine Cavalry. www.state. me.us. An Internet site maintained by the state of Maine.

"General John Buford's Cavalry in the Gettysburg Campaign." www.bufords boys.com. An Internet site on the Union cavalry researched by J. David Petruzzi.

George Kryder Papers www.bgsu.edu. Internet site for the Center for Archival Collections Bowling Green State University.

The History or Biography of J. V. Hoakison During the War of the Rebellion. www.iowa3rdcavalry.com. An Internet site on the Civil War.

Randolph Harrison McKim, *A Soldier's Recollections: Leaves from the Diary of a Young Confederate, with an Oration on the Motives and Aims of the Soldiers of the South.* docsouth.unc.edu.

Electronic edition of a book by the Academic Affairs Library, University of North Carolina at Chapel Hill.

Memoir of Archibald Atkinson Jr. www.scholar2.lib.vt.edu. Virginia Tech University Libraries, Special Collections Department.

New Hampshire Volunteer Cavalry. mem bers.comptek.net. An educational Internet site focusing on the history of the First New Hampshire Cavalry.

A Rebel's Recollections by George Cary Eggleston. docsouth.unc.edu. Electronic edition of a book by the Academic Affairs Library, University of North Carolina at Chapel Hill.

Some Reminiscences by William Lawrence Royall. dcsouth.unc.edu. Electronic edition of a book by the Academic Affairs Library, University of North Carolina at Chapel Hill.

Wartime Diary of John Weatherred. www.jackmasters.net. An Internet site on the cavalry in the Civil War.

War-Time Reminiscences of James D. Sedinger, Company E, 8th Virginia Cavalry (Border Rangers). www.wv-culture.org. The Internet site of the West Virginia State Archives.

INDEX

PICTURE CREDITS

ABOUT THE AUTHOR

Michael V. Uschan has written more than twenty books on a wide variety of historical subjects. He won the Council for Wisconsin Writer's 2001 Juvenile Nonfiction Award for his book *The Korean War.* Uschan began his career as a writer and editor with United Press International, a wire service that provided stories to newspapers, radio, and television. Journalism is sometimes called "history in a hurry." Uschan considers writing history books a natural extension of the research and writing skills he developed as a working journalist. He and his wife, Barbara, reside in the Milwaukee suburb of Franklin, Wisconsin.